KILLING ME SOFTLY

Killing Me Softly

What is love?

Jeanette Shaw

To order additional copies of this book, contact:
Xlibris Corporation
1-888-795-4274
www.Xlibris.com
Orders@Xlibris.com
108918

CONTENTS

CHAPTER 1

Planning Their Lives Together

Like any other young couple growing to love, you may know some that are high school sweethearts. You also have some that remain together for many of years. What will you call a relationship when two people remain together from grade school and still together in the same college, planning their lives together?

Well, my good friend Sheryl and Roger, they are still together after all these years. Just about the time for Sheryl to graduate from the community college in her town, Sheryl and Roger were talking about moving in together; they are the best of friends. What can go wrong?

Sheryl's mother talked her out of moving in with Roger, just until she finished with the community college in their town. She was trying to protect Sheryl from making the same mistakes she did when she was younger and going to college.

It really bothered Sheryl's mother how close she and Roger has become; she knew sex had to be involved.

Six months has passed since they graduated.

Before moving to the state where Roger and Sheryl resides now, they used to live in the country side closer to their families. Sheryl's family never approved of her and Roger's relationship, but that didn't stop her from feeling the way she do about Roger.

Sheryl chose Roger over her family, which in some cases happens all the time between families, maybe they knew something that she didn't, or maybe they just didn't want them together. Sheryl didn't care and decided to move along with Roger. They had no problems in their relationship—hell, they were friends for years, didn't that count for something? Or it just didn't matter to her family?

Seven Years Later

It's now been seven years since Roger and Sheryl moved in together. Sheryl completed college, receiving her Bachelor's degree in psychology and Roger with a business degree now working for what they really believed in. Sheryl worked very hard. She constantly tries to please her boss, to prove to him that she's worthy of managing her own firm. Sheryl knew that there were a lot that has to be done, and proven to show her boss just that.

Her boss would do certain things to Sheryl just to see if she would crack under pressure, or just to see how much load she could carry. Sheryl made no mistakes, she loved challenges and hated to quit anything she started, and she's always been that way, never giving up on anything.

It was a great Tuesday evening. Sheryl didn't expect to be promoted on her job; it was a surprise to her. Roger had a couple of little gigs on the side working as a realtor and a part-time carpenter.

Later that evening, Roger planned a special dinner for the two of them; a candlelight dinner on their balcony, being intimate was also on the menu. Roger and Sheryl, both being busy and loving what they did, never paid any attention to how much sex they had. Once or twice a week was fine with them, neither ever complains. But lately, Roger was looking for more out of Sheryl sexually, but she didn't want sex to be the object of their relationship. Roger got upset at times, but nothing ever separated them. Sheryl loved dealing with people and helping them, so she decided to tutor at a college in the town she lived as she completed her internship in the medical field. Sheryl was working real hard to open her own practice, which means long hours at the office and less time with Roger.

Meals Alone

A couple of month had passed and Roger ate plenty of his meals alone! Should Roger understand that Sheryl's career would be time-consuming and the patients would need her undivided attention? New faces and giving all of the attention he used to get to the clients, Roger began to drift away from Sheryl. Not really noticeable by Sheryl who was busy as she was. Rogers started doing off the wall things to get Sheryl's attention.

Roger had no reason feeling the way he did. They both had positive jobs that required a lot of attention. They both agreed not to have children for the first four years of their careers. Sheryl set up dinner for Roger when she could, and they had always had a great time together. It was always as if they had just met. They were very close and always talked about things that were bothering them or any concerns they may had; they always worked through everything together. Roger stated to Sheryl that he's not getting enough attention from her. Sheryl tried to secure him, letting him know that when you actually start building a career, you have to put a lot of time and effort in it to get promoted to where you need to be.

Roger agreed with Sheryl, but he was still upset. Roger was just being not only selfish but also jealous of the different men that Sheryl was around on a daily basis. Sheryl never gave Roger any doubts about their relationship. With the two of them being together for as long as they had, Roger should be more understanding about Sheryl's career and with their relationship! Why did Roger feel this way? Roger was the only man Sheryl ever wanted. Not saying that she hadn't been approached by all types of men, it would be hard not to approach a beautiful woman as Sheryl. Her honesty and loyalty led her into the arms of one man. What was Roger really scared of? What did Sheryl do to make Roger feel so insecure? Roger started plotting on what he should do to get more of Sheryl's attention.

Chapter 2

Days Home

Sheryl spent quite a few days home during the week now to give Roger more attention he claimed he didn't get. Sheryl agreed to work long hours three days a week and be home no later than five o' clock for the remainder of the week. But that wasn't good enough for Roger. What was it he really wanted? Did someone give him false information about Sheryl? Did he feel as though Sheryl was slipping away from him? What's really going on? Sheryl kept her promise.

Schedule Change

It's been six months since Sheryl made changes to her schedule to give Roger more of her attention. Did that really solve the problem? Was Roger pleased to see that Sheryl cared about how he's feeling? Evidently it didn't. Roger would often play sick when Sheryl had to leave work early at times. Roger thought that this would work in his favor. It might have worked quite a few times with Sheryl, but she caught on to what Roger was doing. She let Roger know that she knew that he wasn't really sick, but she was willing to give him that time he so eagerly wanted from her. She also let him know that she won't have a job if she's not a reliable person.

Roger then came out of the little shell he was in and let Sheryl know that there was too many men around her and that she was giving everyone else all the attention he used to get from her. Sheryl tried to explain to Roger that her career was taking off unless she did her job as ordered or she wouldn't be able to earn her spot in the firm or become a partner, which would qualify her to start her own practice. Roger didn't want to hear that he was only concern about his well-being. At this time, Roger really wanted Sheryl to stay home and be a house wife, but he knew Sheryl would not do such thing. She went to school to get the education and knowledge she needed to be the owner of her own firm one day. Roger was asking for a lot if he would even peruse Sheryl of standing down on what she always wanted to be in her life.

CHAPTER 3

Furious Roger

Roger was furious because his plan didn't work long enough for him; now he's plotting and thinking what he could do to make her stay home while he worked. Sheryl had done all she could to please Roger, but there's nothing more she could do. She had cut her hours at the office for Roger; she's now home between five and five thirty to prepare dinner like he wanted on a daily basis. Roger was just unbelievable; he wanted to watch Sheryl and every move that she made.

Roger was home sitting watching a little TV when a commercial came on showing families with their children playing in the park. What was on Roger's mind at this point? Roger did the unthinkable. He immediately went upstairs to their bedroom, walked into the bathroom, opened the medicine cabinet where Sheryl kept her contraceptives, and Roger decided to tamper with it.

Sheryl came home on a great Thursday evening at about four o'clock and set up a beautiful dinner for Roger. "Wow!" Roger stated. "This is how it should be!"

"What do you mean?" asked Sheryl. "Just to be able to eat dinner together," Roger replied.

Sheryl smiled and told Roger, "Give me a few minutes; I'm going to take a shower. Do you want to join me?"

"No! Go ahead; I'll take one when you're done. I'll just wrap up this paperwork I have here."

"Okay," Sheryl replied.

Contraceptive

Sheryl proceeded to her bedroom stripping off her clothes, getting into the shower. Sheryl had always tried to keep things together, and she would always try to keep the peace and all confusion out of their relationship. As she rinsed the soap off of her back, Roger sneaked in the bathroom to make sure that the diaphragm was where it supposed to be. Roger began to walk out of the bathroom; Sheryl noticed Roger and asked him to hand her, her diaphragm out of the medicine cabinet. He hesitated and then opened the cabinet door, walked toward the shower, slid the door open, and quickly tore the package open for Sheryl. Sheryl didn't think anything of it; she proceeded to put in her diaphragm. Sheryl didn't know that he tampered with something that which was protecting them from having children. The shower turned off. Quickly Roger started to take his clothes off to enter the shower. Sheryl kissed Roger and told him to make it quick so they could spend the rest of the evening together. Sheryl proceeded to the kitchen to prepare the table.

Coffee Shop News

The phone rang. It was one of Sheryl's coworkers Amy, telling her about the lady that just got hired at the coffee shop and had her baby on the job. They didn't know that she was pregnant. "Ooh!" Sheryl said.

"What is it," Amy asked. It reminded Sheryl about her diaphragm. "Oh! I just remembered I did put it in already."

"Wow!" said Amy, "you're very serious about not having kids."

"Yes, I am," said Sheryl. "I have to nail this position. When I do, I will have my own firm."

"I know that's right," stated Amy. "Hey, Sheryl, what is that guy's name that sits next to you at your office, on the left or right?"

"On the right Amy answered?

"Hold on!" Sheryl looked back to make sure that Roger was still in the bathroom. She immediately whispered to Amy, "That is Carl. Please don't ask me about any of the guys on my job, that is a touchy situation for Roger. He has a problem with me working around that many guys on the job."

"Why should he care?" asked Amy. "You love him dearly."

"Well, I don't know," said Sheryl.

"Well, give him my number!"

"Okay, I will. Well, I have to get dinner served. I'll talk to you tomorrow."

"Okay, bye. Sure thing," said Amy. Sheryl felt better that she had her contraceptive in to protect herself from having any children right now. She knew already what was about to take place after dinner.

Sheryl and Roger had a wonderful dinner now sitting by the fireplace drinking champagne. They began to talk about the first time they met and how far they had come. Roger got quiet for a moment, and Sheryl asked him what was wrong. He started on Sheryl about her spending more time with him; he started giving her the sob stories about how much he loves and cares for her. That just hit a spot in Sheryl's heart; she immediately leaned over and kissed Roger, caressing his body, putting him in the mood to forget about him being so lonely.

CHAPTER 4

Making Love

They made love in front of the fireplace and later took it upstairs, more in their comfort zone. Sheryl really gave Roger more than she ever did since they've been together. Roger was really expressing his inner thoughts at this time. "What in the hell had gotten into you tonight?" he asked.

"Are you complaining about something?" asked Sheryl. "No, baby, it's just that you are really putting it down."

"Well, there's more where that came from."

"Wow," stated Roger, "you tired me out, and I have to work in the morning."

"So do I," said Sheryl.

"Let's get some rest. I really enjoy you tonight. Thanks for a great meal and a wonderful night." They kissed each other. Later they both were sound asleep. It was about three in the morning when Roger got up for a glass of water. He then returned to the bedroom staring at Sheryl, really regretting what he had done, but he couldn't take it back. What's done was done. Roger kindly let up on Sheryl about her hours at work because he felt guilty really wanting to tell her a couple of time but didn't know how to start the conversation. Often shows may come on TV while he was eating dinner and Roger would often comment on the family thing. He would ask Sheryl when she would be ready to start a family.

Her answer was always not right now, and that would usually be the end of conversation. Not this time, Roger made a remark, "I would love a son!" Sheryl then told Roger, "We both are real busy, what we are going do if I stop working to have a kid? My career just took off, and I'm working on my own practice right now. That's just not a good idea. Not right now, maybe after a year or two of marriage." That wasn't a good answer for Roger; he then got up from the dinner table upset at the answer Sheryl gave him.

"I need some air," Roger stated.

Roger began walking out the front door. Sheryl went behind him. "Where are you going?" Roger replied, "To the bar? I need a drink or two."

"Honey, do not drink and drive. We have plenty to drink here," said Sheryl.

"Yeah, yeah," said Roger. "I need to get some air." Roger stayed out for a couple of hours. When he returned, Sheryl was asleep. Roger was furious with Sheryl. The conversation of having children didn't come up again for several weeks. They both woke up the same time every morning for work. Roger didn't feel great. He wasn't sure if he could make it into work. He thought maybe he drank too much liquor at the bar the night before. Sheryl never saw Roger like this ever. She made sure that he was okay before she left for work; she asked him if he wanted her to stay home. He said he would be fine, that he was going to work a little late. Sheryl got to her office and started her day. Roger went to work but came home early still not feeling very well. Three days had passed, and things seemed to be going just fine as of now. Sheryl got up for work, and Roger was constantly going in late.

Checking on Roger

Sheryl called Roger around twelve thirty, and he answered the home phone. "Roger, I thought you were going to work?"

"I was," answered Roger, "but I feel like a dog. I don't think I will make it in today."

"Okay, well, I'll see you at home, honey, I'll be there a little early," said Sheryl. She hung up the phone and took care of her patients. Sheryl was home by four o'clock. Sheryl walked in the house, and as she walked upstairs, she heard a gasping sound in the bathroom. Sheryl quickly ran up to Roger. "Honey, are you all right?" Roger was purging in the sink. "I don't feel too well."

"Did you have anything to eat today?" asked Sheryl.

"I tried, but I couldn't keep anything down."

"Let's go to the Doctor, you may have gotten into some bad liquor."

"No! I don't need a doctor. I need to lie down."

Roger tried lying down for an hour, but he couldn't. Every fifteen minutes, he's purging and purging. "That's it," said Sheryl. "Let's go. I'm taking you to the doctor's office to get you checked out."

Sheryl took Roger to the emergency room. It took a while for Roger to be seen.

After three hours, the doctor came in and let Sheryl and Roger know it was nothing serious. It might just be a bug going around, and they just needed to see his private doctor in the next few days. Roger was out of work for three straight days.

CHAPTER 5

Back to Work

Sheryl couldn't figure out what was wrong with Roger. The following week, Roger felt a little better. He was able to go to work but still felt bad. A few months had passed, Sheryl was now traveling out of the country for her patients, but she constantly checked on Roger. Roger finally decided to go to get an overall check-up from his doctor because it had been four and a half months and he still felt nauseated. They didn't find anything, Roger was perfectly healthy. What could Roger be allergic to? Roger couldn't figure out why he felt so sick.

Roger told Sheryl that he needed her there with him, but Sheryl won't be back in town for the next week or so. Roger was not happy about that. Sheryl's internship had started, and she had to spend more time out of town then home with Roger. She really worked it out and changed her schedule to please Roger for the last several months, but he just wouldn't compromise with what Sheryl wanted. Sheryl was trying everything to please Roger. Roger was now carrying all the sickness Sheryl was supposed to be carrying. Roger felt okay at times, but had these queasy feelings late at night.

Roger, feeling the way he do, really didn't feel like arguing about Sheryl's trips back and forth out of town. He's feeling as though Sheryl was neglecting him. But he had no reason to think this way. Sheryl practically changed her whole life for Roger, what more could he want?

Hanging Out

Roger is now hanging out with his friends at the bar, coming in late at night, wanting to have sex with Sheryl, after all that drinking and smelling the way he did. Sheryl refused to have sex with Roger not only because of him being drunk but also because it's three in the morning and she had to go to work the next morning. "Why don't you want to have sex with me? Don't answer that, I know why," he said with a slur in his voice. "Since you've been going out of town, we haven't been doing much of nothing."

"Roger, what are you saying?" Sheryl asked.

"Who is he?" Roger asked. "Is it your boss?" he demanded to know.

"Roger, I will not sit here and argue with you about this. You know I work, when do I have time for another man? I am trying to start my own practice in less than a year. I have to go on some trips with my colleagues. Do you understand that?"

Roger had a bad attitude and thought negative thoughts about Sheryl after all these years. How could Roger ever doubt Sheryl? She never gave him a reason to think that way. Roger doubting Sheryl was really hurting their relationship. As time passed by, he now had company over three days a week, late at night playing cards and drinking, something he didn't do except on occasions. Sheryl's boss wanted her to go on special ops three months prior, but she turned it down to please Roger.

CHAPTER 6

Roger Changes

Now that Roger was changing and not having much respect for Sheryl, she decided not only to comply with the special ops assignments her boss gave her but also thought it was a good time for her to go away for a while and think things through concerning where the relationship was going. Sheryl talked to Roger about going on the special ops that night at the dinner table; she let him know that these ops would consist of forty-five days out of town. She offered him to come spend three days a week with her, but being that his job was demanding, he couldn't go. He told Sheryl flat out no. That she couldn't go. Sheryl screamed at Roger, "You know, I have had enough of this. I'm not a kid; I don't need your permission. I have done a lot of turndowns on my job to please you, and you think I'm sleeping with my boss. If you keep accusing me, I may just do it." Roger leapt across the table and slapped Sheryl.

"Roger! What has gotten into you, why did you do that?" Sheryl was scared out of her mind.

Roger quickly replied, "I'm sorry, I wasn't thinking." Sheryl got up from the table holding the left side of her face and continued to walk upstairs crying. Roger went upstairs behind her.

"Get away from me, Roger, what's gotten into you?" she sobbed.

"I'm sorry, baby," said Roger.

"You know, Roger, this maybe a good time for me to go. I think things are over between us. We have been together for fourteen and a half years. I've never cheated on you or looked at another man. I will be leaving in two weeks for my trip," she stated.

"Sheryl, you really don't need to go for that long, you know I don't feel well. I need you here with me," Roger pleaded.

"Yes! Roger, you really showed me how much you need me here." Sheryl walked off. As she walked off, she felt queasy and had to lie down for a few minutes.

"What's wrong?" Roger asked. "I'm fine," said Sheryl.

Five and a half months had passed and Sheryl still had no symptoms whatsoever. She gained only seven pounds but nothing that was questionable to Roger. It's now closer to Sheryl leaving, just a couple of days. Roger was now hanging close to home with Sheryl. Feeling sorry for what he did, knowing that Sheryl would be boarding her plane within the next forty-eight hours.

Roger tried to talk her out of it, but Sheryl had already decided on going. She really needed a break from Roger. Roger offered to spend that whole evening with Sheryl, not going to work, and offered to cook dinner for the two of them. Sheryl agreed to Roger cooking a meal for them that evening. Roger decided to cook steak, mash potato gravy, corn, and, he knew her favorite food in the world, shrimps.

Roger couldn't get Sheryl to change her mind about going out of town on this trip. Roger had to think of something that would prohibit Sheryl from leaving home. Roger was pacing the floor down in the basement beating his brain on what he could do to make Sheryl stay home.

You Make Me Sick

Roger did the unthinkable. Roger decided to cook Sheryl food and placed a large amount of antidepressant in it, something she had an allergic reaction to earlier that month. Sheryl didn't feel anything unusual, just a slight headache. They finished the evening out; Sheryl went upstairs to pack her bags to leave out at five in the morning. It was about one in the morning. Sheryl jumped out of bed and ran to the bathroom. Her stomach was very upset she purged twice. She didn't know what was happening. She didn't think anything of it, so she just cleaned herself up and went back to bed. Roger asked Sheryl, "Are you all right?"

"Yes, I just felt woozy for a minute." Early that morning Sheryl got up and got her bags together for her trip. Roger expected Sheryl to be in pain.

He asked Sheryl, "How you are feeling?" She replied to Roger, "I feel great! Better than I did last night."

Well, it's time for Sheryl to go. Roger was very upset because his plan didn't work. Sheryl was now leaving for her forty-five-day trip. She expected to land at 1:30 p.m. She made it to the Sheraton Hotel where she would be staying for four days, and then she would be taking off to Chicago. She had six patients there. Sheryl called Roger to let him know that everything was fine and she would talk to him later that night.

Sheryl saw two of her patients there so far. She began to feel very sick. Sheryl couldn't see anyone else that day. She decided to go to her room and rest for the rest of the day and start fresh in the morning. Sheryl didn't place that call to Roger like she said. He immediately thought negative things, so he called Sheryl's room. She answered on the fourth ring. Sheryl answered the phone like she was down and out. "Why are you talking like that?" asked Roger. "I don't feel well at all."

"Why, what's wrong?" Roger asked.

"I really don't know."

"Maybe you need to come home, Sheryl."

"Well, if I don't feel any better in the next hour or two, I will take a flight out tomorrow. Right now, I feel so bad I can't finish my day, I can't get back out of the bed."

"Do you need me to come get you?"

"No," answered Sheryl. "I'll just call my boss and let him know that I won't be making it in and I may have to go home."

"Okay," said Roger. Roger thought his plan was working for him and that he would see Sheryl later that night, but Sheryl felt a little better enough to see a couple of patients that evening.

Unfinished Business

Sheryl made it two and a half weeks in Chicago. She's now fatigue. Sheryl decided she was going home the next day. She didn't finish her internship, but with the effort Sheryl made for this company throughout the years, her boss was satisfied with her work, so he promoted her. Sheryl knew nothing about it.

Sheryl's colleagues wanted to take her out before she went back home being it was her last night there. They decided to go to the bar and grill down from the hotel. They grabbed a bite to eat and drank one glass of wine. That was a bad idea for Sheryl. That made her stomach do a three sixty on her. She felt some of everything, but she thought it was all gas. They had ended the night after Sheryl took sick. They walked her to her room and offered to sit with her for a little while. But Sheryl declined and told them that she would be fine and that she would see them back home. Roger knew that Sheryl would be coming home, and he expected her no later than nine thirty a.m. Sheryl felt bad, but she didn't catch a cab to go home. After getting off the plane, she went straight to the office. Roger must not have checked his phone last night when Sheryl left a message that she would be going straight to the office when she gets off the plane. It's about 11:00 a.m., Sheryl's almost at the office. Roger finally checked his voicemail, and he heard the message and quickly ran to his car and headed to the office where Sheryl was. Sheryl just made it to her office, walking upstairs. She saw a lot of balloons, food, cake, drinks, and a lot of people mingling; and she didn't think anything of it, maybe just someone's birthday party.

The Promotion

Her boss called her on the loudspeaker to come to his office. While walking toward his office, her boss met her in the hall, leading her to where everyone was. Just as Roger walked in, Sheryl's boss announced that Sheryl had completed her internship and she's now partners with the firm and she's also eligible for her own practice if she decides.

Sheryl didn't feel well, but she shed a few tears and began to hug all of her colleagues. Her boss embraced her with a big hug and a kiss on both sides of the cheek. Roger was furious; he didn't know that Sheryl worked around young students from the college she tutors from time to time.

Plenty of men at the office, alone and single! He had this jealous look on his face. Sheryl didn't know that Roger was there just yet.

CHAPTER 7

Sheryl's Promotion Party

Sheryl started giving thanks, to her coworkers, friends, her boss, and God for bringing her this far. She named all of the people that she wanted to work with when she opens her practice. Sheryl had four men in mind; two of them were at the ages of twenty-seven, Keith, and thirty-year-old Danny. Sheryl chose them because they would need to service three hundred hours intern to be hired at her firm, and she could use the funding that was paid for them to participate.

Andrew was forty-two, and he knew Roger, but Sheryl had no recollection of that. Earl, age forty-eight and sexy as can be, was a strong person that Sheryl needed on her side.

Quite frankly, Roger didn't care for Andrew at all. Amy, being older than Sheryl and who trained her, wanted no longer to work for the firm; she wanted to work for Sheryl. And there's Tory, age twenty-eight. Sheryl didn't know her that well, but she was always on time and made her job her first priority.

Roger was sitting in the back about to blow up. One of her colleagues let her know that Roger was sitting in the back. She told Angie to tell him to come up, and he did. She stayed about an hour and a half, and she left to go home, letting everyone know that she didn't feel well. As Roger and Sheryl were leaving, she was beginning to lose her balance. Sheryl stated that she really needed to sit down for a minute. Her legs were kind of weak. He held her up and said, "Come on, we're almost to the car."

Roger said to Sheryl, "You didn't tell me anything about the ceremony today." Roger was upset. "How can I tell you what I didn't know?" she hissed, still feeling bad. "How did you not know?" Roger got a little loud. "I didn't finish my clients, but it's my boss's decision. He decided that I have plenty of hours in to graduate early." Roger asked Sheryl, "So with this promotion, will this have you travelling more than usual?" Roger asked, hoping she would say no. "Well, yes?" answered Sheryl. "And now I will be on my own, I will be training interns at my office. I will have to travel a lot, more than usual."

"How often" Roger asked.

"That's really up to the company and how much patients I need to see. Whatever my secretary books me for during the week, I will have to do," Sheryl replied.

"Well, I don't like it," said Roger.

"Where's this coming from, Roger?" She wanted to know.

"That's a stupid question, Sheryl," said Roger.

"Roger, you know what my job is consisting of." Sheryl took a deep breath, she felt really bad. She began to yell, "Look, Roger! I don't feel well at all, we can discuss this later."

"No!" Roger shouted. "We will discuss this now." Roger pulled into the driveway.

Sheryl replied in a weak voice, "Look, Roger, I really need to lie down. I don't feel like talking right now."

The Violence

Roger pulled into the garage. Sheryl got out of the car and went to the door, sticking the key into the door. Roger yelled, "Sheryl." Sheryl didn't answer him. She continued to open the door and went inside. "You didn't hear me?" asked Roger. "You do everything for your boss; you hear everything he had to say."

"That's my job," responded Sheryl.

With greater anger, Roger asked, "What did you say?" He slapped Sheryl without realizing how much anger he had inside of him. Being as weak as she was and feeling sick, Sheryl fell down to her knees. She couldn't move at the moment; she slowly pried herself up against the wall.

"I'm sorry," said Roger.

"I heard that before." While whipping her mouth, she said to Roger, "To tell you the truth, I've heard sorry all my life. You know what, I'm tired of hearing it, and you're not sorry at all. This is not the first time you put your hands on me." He tried to help her up the stairs. "Don't touch me," Sheryl shouted. She hurled on the fourth step going up. Roger had no idea what was wrong with Sheryl. Pregnancy was out of his mind. It had been six months and Roger expected a woman to be sick in the first few weeks of pregnancy. His cell phone rang. He looked at the caller ID, but he didn't pick up. Sheryl didn't make it to the shower; she fell in the bed with no response.

Roger walked in the room just moments later, sitting on the edge of the bed, telling Sheryl how sorry he was and that it wouldn't happen again. He continued to tell her how jealous he was feeling and he shouldn't feel that way. He asked her to forgive him. Sheryl didn't respond. He called out to her, still no response. He shook Sheryl, still no movement. He constantly called out to her and finally turned her over. Her lips looked pale. He lifted her up, screaming, "Sheryl! Oh my god, what have I done? Sheryl, I'm sorry baby, please wake up."

Roger continued calling her name and lifted her up, but Sheryl didn't respond. "Sheryl, I didn't mean it, please." Roger called nine one, one and told them that "Sheryl is not responding, I'm trying to awake her, but she's not moving at all."

"Do you know what happen to her, sir?"

"Well, we just came in from her office, and she got off the plane today and went to the office. She said she was sick for a couple of weeks when she was out of town. We just walked in, and she lay on the bed. I came in just minutes later. I was talking to her. When she didn't respond the second time, I went over to the bed and rolled her over, calling her. Still no answer"

Hospitalized

The ambulance arrived at the house. They quickly rushed Sheryl to the hospital, not knowing what was really going on with her. She's barely responding.

When Sheryl arrived at the hospital, they immediately took blood and started an IV. Not only was she dehydrated, but also her blood pressure was sky-high. Dr. Filch came in to get more information about what happened before Sheryl got sick. Roger couldn't really answer any question, and what really covered him was that Sheryl was out of town for a couple of weeks. That's the only thing he would tell the doctor. He didn't let them know that they had an argument or that he struck Sheryl. He didn't say anything else. He let the doctor feed him information of what their findings of Sheryl. It was about an hour when Dr. Filch came back in along with Dr. Rainy, a gynecologist from a private practice. Sheryl was stable but asleep at this point. Roger, with his mind rattled at this point, did not question why Sheryl would need a gynecologist; it's still far from his mind about pregnancy.

CHAPTER 8

Test Results

The doctor talked to Roger and let him know that they had found the results of her test, and he asked Roger, "Did she eat anything that she might have been allergic to because it seemed that her body had responded to something bad? And of course, other test result we have to discuss with her when she awakes." They wanted to see what Sheryl was taking that could have caused her to pass out and become sick as she did. Being that, she didn't have a history of sickness in the family, so the doctors were puzzled. They didn't let Roger know about the pregnancy. They wanted to tell Sheryl firsthand. News travels fast, and all of the coworkers from the office that knew Sheryl were at the hospital in the waiting room, waiting for Sheryl to wake up so they could see her and let her know that they were there for her. It wasn't long before Sheryl awoke.

"What happened? Where am I?"

"You're at the hospital, Sheryl."

"What happened?"

"You got sick and passed out."

"Why, what happened?"

Dr. Rainy told Roger that he had to leave the room for a few minutes. Roger asked why. "It's protocol. We have to do that when we believe that a patient has been poisoned."

"What?" said Sheryl?

"You may come in later; we'll talk to you then."

"No! What do you mean when someone has been poisoned? What are you talking about?"

"We will explain that to you in just a moment, but it's mandatory that we speak with Sheryl right now." The doctor wanted to ask Sheryl some questions concerning Roger and their relationship. The doctor also asked her about any vitamins that she might have been taking. Sheryl told the doctor that she left the bottle at home and she only took nine pills since she's been out of town. Dr. Filch told Sheryl that he needed the pill bottle from her home to get them down to the lab; the extensiveness of her blood work showed them that there's no way that she could have these high test numbers without it being forced or with someone who wanted to commit suicide.

The doctor also let her know that vitamins, even if she took six in one day, would not have toxin in our system. Sheryl immediately told Roger to go home and get the pill bottle for the doctor. It didn't take Roger thirty minutes; he took the pills down to the lab where they began to check the vitamin pills Sheryl was taking. Dr. Filch stepped in and introduced Dr. Rainy. Sheryl immediately asked Dr. Filch why her gynecologist is here. She asked him why she needed to see a gynecologist. Dr. Rainy told Sheryl that she was pregnant.

"Pregnant? I can't have any kids right now, I just can't. Is it too late for an abortion? Did you tell Roger?"

"No, we didn't tell him about the pregnancy. That may have been the cause of you passing out and getting sick, and what may have triggered it may have been the pills you were taking. Did you have any of sickness that may have given you an idea that you may have been pregnant?"

"No, I'm fine. I was never sick until now. I was going out of town on a regular basis. It's nothing. I just wasn't sick at all. Tell me what I can do! I can't have a baby."

"Well," said Dr. Rainy, "Sheryl, I'm very sorry, but you are too far gone to be talking about an abortion."

"What do you mean by too far gone? How far are you saying?"

"Well, Sheryl, you are almost seven months, that's twenty-seven weeks to be exact."

"But I have no stomach, just bigger breast, more thickly in the waist, and a little belly, but I've always had that bulge. I have no kind of sickness whatsoever." The doctor assured Sheryl that it happens sometimes in life that a lot of women don't know.

"We will keep you here for a day or two, just to run more test to make sure that the baby is fine." The nurse walked in with the results as the doctor was about to leave.

"You got to see this," they whispered in the corner. "Look at these numbers, there's no way possible she's still breathing with this amount of poison in her system. We have to do something now. Give her a stress test to see if the baby is okay, we need to pump her quickly before it's really too late. We really have to find out what else she has in her home besides these pills."

The nurse said that she would go to the waiting area to tell Roger to bring all of the medication down to the hospital. Sheryl's gynecologist said, "No, this had to be induced so we can't take any chances with him going."

"Well, how would we get it? We have to tell Sheryl what's going on maybe, she can get a family member to retrieve it."

"Sheryl, do you have anyone besides Roger that can retrieve all medication in your home?"

"Why?" asked Sheryl.

"Well, what we found in your system will truly hurt you in the next few hours, and until we can get the actual medication that caused this, we don't know how to treat you, this is very serious."

"Why can't Roger go and get it for you?"

"Sheryl, this medication had to be induced through foods or liquid, we just have to take precautions. We don't want to get the police involved. So please we are not saying that he's done it, but no one who lives in the home needs to retrieve this."

Sheryl sat and thought for a minute. "Well, my colleague Earl is in the waiting room, I'll give him the keys, but Roger can't know about this."

"Hand me the keys, and I'll call Roger back to keep you company so I can give Earl the keys." Dr. Filch walked out and told Roger he can go in to see Sheryl now. Sheryl knowing Roger for as long as she did never thought that Roger had done this. So that's not on her mind at this point.

Frantic

Sheryl was screaming and crying. "Calm down, Sheryl, we are trying to get your pressure down. We can't have you getting upset right now, so please calm down."

"Okay," said Sheryl. Finally, they let Roger know what was going on and that Sheryl was pregnant and had been for a while. He was now concerned and thinking about what he had done to her and their unborn child. Roger loved the sound of pregnancy. But Sheryl wasn't happy at all.

They allowed a few of Sheryl's coworkers to go see her in her room. There were more than ten of them there at once. Roger, wanting to be the center of attention, was getting upset because of the attention Sheryl was getting and everyone was by passing him like he wasn't even there. Roger was getting furious, so he called Dr. Filch to the side and told him, "If it's just poison, why can't you just flush her system out so she can go home?"

Dr. Filch said to Roger, "I could!"

Roger said, "Great."

"But I won't," stated Dr. Filch. "It's her health and the health of her unborn child is what I'm concern about, Sheryl is very sick, and her life is in danger if we don't do anything in the next few hours." Roger got very irritated with the doctor. He was very upset to the point where they had to call security to remove Roger from the hall to the waiting area. Sheryl heard the commotion down the hall and asked what was going on. They let Sheryl know that Roger was disturbing the hospital and that he wanted her to go home.

Sheryl then asked the doctor, "Why I can't go home?"

Dr. Filch respond, "Well, it's more complicated than you think it is. The test came back positive that the medication you were taking took some negative effects on you, but it wasn't the vitamins, and it has to be flushed out of your system before we can let you leave. If you were not pregnant, you may go earlier. But we have to take precaution for the baby. Being that you are almost seven months pregnant . . ."

"I don't need any kids right now." Sheryl was crying, wanting what the doctors told her to be a dream.

"Sheryl, you have dilated two centimeters. We really have to watch that for the next twenty-four hours."

They finally let Roger in the room to see Sheryl. "God!" she cried with tears coming down her face.

"What's wrong?" Roger asked with a smirk on his face.

"You know we have agreed on no kids for the first four years of marriage, we're not even married yet. How could this have happened? I was always careful. For the last ten years, I have never made a mistake. Roger, you know what we agreed on. My job is taking off, I'm not married, what will I do with a child?"

"Well, marry me then."

Sheryl replied, "What? I will not marry you because of a baby. We have been together for over fourteen years; you have never talked about or asked me about marriage. Why now? I can't think right now, Roger. Please go home and get some rest. Go, Roger, please!"

Roger said fine and left, but Roger didn't go home. He went straight to the bar.

Sheryl continued to cry after the doctor told her about her pregnancy. Dr. Rainy entered the room to let Sheryl know they would have to remove her diaphragm, which may be infected or might cause an infection, being that she's already pregnant. When the doctor removed the diaphragm, he saw that the diaphragm wasn't how it should be and questioned Sheryl about it. Sheryl didn't have any idea what to think because that was just far from her mind, that anyone would do that.

Calling Roger

She wanted Roger to know what was going on, so she called Roger. He was still at the pub with his friends. With the phone on auto-answer, Roger didn't hear the phone ring. Sheryl listened to the conversations Roger was having with one of his friends. Sheryl heard when Roger said he wanted kids and he did what he had to do, and if he didn't do it, he might lose Sheryl. "No!" his friend responded! "Sheryl loves you. What reason does she have to leave you?"

"I messed up, okay, I just messed up."

"How do you mean you messed up? Don't worry about it, man. I'll talk to you later. Okay, call me in the morning." Sheryl hung up the phone; she instantly knew what happened to her diaphragm after hanging up the phone. She turned on the TV. The last thing she wanted to see was kids. She continued to look at the families that really had it together, and they worked and were very happy. Sheryl saw how the fathers were with their children; she started to cry looking at the happy family. Could this be a change of heart for Sheryl?

She picked up the phone to call Roger. When she heard his voice, she hung up the phone. She had mixed feelings knowing what Roger has done and looking at families that have a steady life with children that seemed to be happy. The doctors came back into Sheryl's room and let her know that they found the problem. It was some antidepressant which was in her sleeping pills bottle that didn't belong there. It was mixed with her other pills, which may have caused her to be as sick as she was. He gave Sheryl the bottle and asked her how many pills she had taken. She responded and told the doctor that she didn't take any of that particular one that was a new bottle.

"Well, Sheryl, there are nine pills missing from this bottle. Could you tell me how it got into your system if you didn't take it yourself?"

"I don't know; please tell me that you don't think that Roger did this."

"Who else lives in your home with you?"

"Well, no one."

"We have to report this."

"No," said Sheryl. "Please not right now, give me a couple of weeks, we can't do that."

"We will lose our license; this has to be reported as soon as possible."

Dr. Reese said, "Here I'll handle it from here, I'll take full responsibility."

"Okay, but this will be on you. Is there any reason of you wanting to wait to expose him?"

Sheryl looked at the doctors and said, "Yes, Doc, please bear with me for just a few weeks. It's for security reasons. Look, I promise you, I will cover all of you please."

The doctor was able to give Sheryl the right medication that would flush the poison out her system. It was a little painful, but it's something they had to do or they might have lost them both. Dr. Filch let Sheryl know that she would be feeling bad for a few days more, and she might bleed. "But don't be alarmed, except only if it's bright red and won't stop."

Sheryl was released two days later. Roger continued working. He had no idea that Sheryl was being released. She didn't call Roger to pick her up. Roger had already left work to go home to take a shower so he could go to the hospital to see Sheryl. Sheryl got a cab home; Sheryl was now thinking about what she's going to do, thinking back on that lovely night they shared before she left to go out of town. She remembered getting sick. Now Sheryl had a plan of her own. She got out the cab and went into the house. Roger, already dressed and ready to go to the hospital, walked downstairs and saw Sheryl standing there. Tears just rolled down his face. Roger immediately went to hug Sheryl. Roger then fell to his knees, saying, "Sheryl baby, I'm so sorry, I messed up. Please don't leave me, I didn't mean to do it."

"What are you talking about, Roger? Are you cheating on me?"

"No, baby, I have never cheated since we've been together. I've always been faithful to you, I love you so much. I know we agreed not to have children, but I always wanted a son."

"Stop," Sheryl said, "I know what you did, Roger, and you were wrong. It's very wrong, anything could have happened. We don't have time to plan anything because I'm already going on seven months. I have to start planning for a new life." That sounded so good to Roger, but Sheryl was not speaking about a new life because of them becoming parents with a new addition to the family. Roger didn't know what Sheryl was about to do. Why was he so happy? Do you really think that you can deceive someone and get away with it? Of course not!

CHAPTER 9

Control

Roger told her not to worry, that he would take care of everything. Sheryl responded, "That is the problem you, you want to take care of everything. You want to rule me, be in charge of me, just guide my every move, and control my career. No! That won't happen. I worked very hard to get where I am."

"I love you, Sheryl, will you marry me?"

"No, Roger, and I feel as though you asked me that because of a child."

"Well, don't you love me?"

"What's love got to do with it? You know why I'm in this predicament now, because of you and your selfishness. How can I trust you if you can do something like that? I need time to think."

"What are you saying, Sheryl? Are you having second thoughts about us?"

Sheryl walked away and screamed at Roger, "Sleep downstairs tonight."

"Sheryl, please. Can I talk to you for a minute, please, just give me a minute."

"Fine, what do you have to say to me that might mean something?"

Roger fell to his knees with tears in his eyes and said to Sheryl, "We're not getting any younger. I really love you, and we have been together for fifteen years. I will never hurt you again, I promise you that."

"I can't answer that right now, Roger. I have to think about a lot that will be going on in the next six weeks. I don't have any family here. I have to think of a daycare center for the child. Did you really expect me to stay home and babysit when I have a demanding job and children that needs my attention?

I've been out of work for the last two weeks, how do you think I feel staying home while you're out there working?"

Roger stated to Sheryl, "Well, that is my job."

"Your job!" said Sheryl. "What about my job? Is that not important to you? I have nothing else to say, Roger. I'm going to take a shower and lie down." So Sheryl walked away. Roger was now furious with Sheryl because once again, he couldn't have his way.

Roger decided he want to go to the bar with his friends to have a couple of drinks. Roger made it a habit of going to the bar with his friends when he's upset or couldn't have his way for the last four months. He's coming in the house after two and three in the morning. Sheryl asked Roger what was really out there that time of the morning for him to be staying out this late. "Why don't you drink in the privacy of your own home?" Not only was Roger staying out late, but he now also had two to three nights a week when his friends come over to the house. Sheryl didn't mind his company coming over, but they were doing it in a very disrespectful way. Roger's company got drunk, had loud cursing going on, sometimes invited their female friends over while Sheryl was in her bed. It could get very loud, and Sheryl didn't have many weeks left and she's very cranky. Sheryl proceeded to go downstairs. She didn't know that Roger had allowed his friends to invite girls over to their house while she was asleep. Sheryl walked down the stairs. No one could hear her coming down because of the loud noise going on in the dining area.

Sheryl got to the dining area. She saw one girl sitting on her table. "What the fuck are you doing? Sheryl screamed at the young lady whom was sitting on her table saying if you don't get your funky ass off my table, pregnant or not, I'll whip your ass. Roger, Sheryl called out his name asking him what in the hell do you mean? None of you have respect. It's two o' clock in the goddamned morning. Drinking, cursing, and having these bitches up in my house this time in the morning while I'm in my bed. I don't think so, Roger."

Party Is Over

"This party is over. Everybody out you bunch of hooch's. Don't ever come back to my house again."

Roger made a statement, "That's my boy, girlfriend."

Sheryl said, "I'll tell you what. Pack your bag and go with them. How about that? Roger, this has been going on too long. What respect are you showing me in this house?"

Roger said with his smart-ass mouth, "You know a man got to hold on to his brief around their friends."

He told Sheryl, "I pay the damn bills, so what are you saying I can't have my friends over to my own damn house?"

"Your house"

"Yes, My house?"

"I'm taking care of home and taking care of you. So you have a lot to say in front of your friends, right, Roger? You have changed a lot."

"Yes, you have changed me!" said Roger. Sheryl walked off went back upstairs in the bed. She really didn't feel like arguing with Roger.

Sheryl thought Roger just let his friends out and lay down on the sofa in the den. But Roger went with them to the pub two miles down, not far from their house. One of Sheryl's coworkers called her and told her that she and her husband were at the pub and they saw Roger and his friends sitting with four women at the table. Sheryl was informed that the strip show would start in thirty minutes. Sheryl kindly put on something nice and revealing and didn't have to worry about clothes. Her stomach didn't show as if she were not pregnant. She made her way down to the bar, and lo and behold, Roger was getting a lap dance from the same young lady that just left their house. *So he's bringing strippers to our home.* Sheryl went in and sat by her friends for a good fifteen minutes. Roger was so into what he was doing he didn't realize that they all were sitting there looking at him. He was all into the girls, passing out plenty of money. Touching their breasts and their buttocks! Sheryl saw enough and left. She went home like nothing ever happened. Sheryl really made up in her mind that she was going to leave; she had to get some things in order. Sheryl played it really smart; she treated Roger like she always did. Sheryl never spent a dime out of her bank account except for the small things she might buy when she's out.

The Account

Sheryl had an account that Roger knew nothing about. One of the accounts that Sheryl had was from her firm that she worked for, and the one she used to deposit her sign-on bonus that the firm gave her, which was two hundred and fifty-five thousand dollars. With that deposit and seven years' worth of deposits, Sheryl now had eight hundred and ninety-five thousand in that account. She bought stocks and bonds Roger knew nothing about. Sheryl learned from her mother's experience. Her mother had a good man like Roger, but at the end, it was hell and no one had believed he was that person. So Sheryl, with no doubt, protected herself.

While Roger was sitting there thinking that Sheryl needed him financially, the truth was she really didn't. Roger thought that Sheryl had only ninety-six thousand dollars in her main account plus what they had together. Sheryl was not allowed to withdraw any money without the bank calling Roger first. So for the last three years, Sheryl has been pinching and pinching and got enough for her to be comfortable.

It's now four thirty in the morning. Roger came in past drunk, wanting to get in the bed with Sheryl. "No!" Sheryl said. "You're stinking! Get out."

"No! This is my bed too."

"Well, you can have it. I'm just sick of this."

Roger told Sheryl, "Go ahead downstairs then. Help yourself, shit!"

"Whatever!" Sheryl slept on the couch. She got up early that morning to get some things in order. Sheryl needed a break from Roger, so she decided to call her old boss to see if he had anything that was far away so she could leave town and make it a vacation at the same time away from Roger.

CHAPTER 10

Leaving

Sheryl's in luck! Her boss had two states that Sheryl could visit. Sheryl would be traveling to Michigan once again for two days and then to the island in Jamaica for one week. Sheryl was told by her doctor that it would be fine to travel, but not out of the country. Sheryl knew she had a slim chance being that she only had six weeks left before her delivery. Sheryl said not one word to Roger. She's not leaving for another three days. Sheryl played it safe, and she packed her suitcases with everything she could possibly need for a trip for two whole weeks. She put it in the trunk of her car in the garage. Sheryl made dinner, hoping that she could have at least one or two sensible days out of the week with Roger. Roger never came home after work. He and his friends went to the bar after work.

Sheryl ate dinner alone and put Roger's food in the oven, leaving a note on the table to let him know that. Roger decided to come home, and it's already one forty-five in the morning. He didn't come alone. He came with four of his male friends and two females, but later, there were more. "Here we go again." Sheryl's having her natural Braxton Hicks contraction, which was normal. Not feeling like being bothered or having any sorts of noise, Roger decided he wanted to play card and drink all night with his friends. Sheryl put up with Roger and all the noise they had going on for the last two hours.

Sheryl decided to go downstairs. She called Roger. Roger didn't hear her because of all the noise downstairs. Sheryl was very tired, more than usual. Sheryl continued to walk downstairs. She got to the bottom of the stairs and yelled, "Roger . . ."

"What!" Roger answered.

"Could you all keep it down, I'm trying to sleep."

Roger got up from the table and walked toward Sheryl. Roger asked Sheryl, "What did you said to me?" Sheryl repeated what she said the first time. Roger bent over and whispered in Sheryl's ear, "Don't you ever try to embarrass me like that in front of my friends ever again! I pay the damn bills in this house."

Sheryl, with her mouth slightly opened, said, "Roger."

He responded, "Don't Roger me." Sheryl asked Roger why he was speaking to her that way. Roger said to Sheryl, "Go back to bed; it's just us boys out here." Immediately after Roger said "It was just us boys," Sheryl heard two girls laughing in her kitchen. She pretended like she didn't hear them. Roger continued to tell Sheryl, "Go, go back to bed." Sheryl walked off with tears in her eyes. She went up the step as fast as she could, but those pains hit her kind of hard. She paused for a few minutes.

Roger didn't even offer to help her upstairs. The pain was beating Sheryl all around the stomach area. Finally Sheryl made it upstairs; she sat on the bed for a few minutes then decided to take a warm bath. Roger heard the water running, so he decided to go upstairs in the bathroom where Sheryl was. He asked Sheryl, "Why are you taking another bath?" She just looked at him and didn't answer him. He repeated the question, but in a stronger tone.

Sheryl asked Roger, "What is wrong with you? You are drinking too much. I really don't feel well and don't feel like talking. I felt like a warm bath, so I'm taking one, or do you own that too? You know, Roger, you have changed for the worst."

The Disrespect

"You treat me different because I'm not working and really can't do much around here. You really treat me like a dog. I thought we were better than this, you don't respect me anymore." Roger walked out and slammed the door. Sheryl proceeded with her bath. The noise had gotten louder. *I can't do this anymore*, Sheryl said to herself. Sheryl got out of the tub and dried off. She took out an overnight bag. *That's enough; I can't have peace in my own home anymore.* She began to cry looking back on the life she thought she and Roger had all these years. Sheryl questioned herself what she had done to cause Roger to change after all these years together. *I've given him everything, what could have gone wrong?*

Sheryl packed a few things for just the night. Roger still knew nothing about the luggage she had packed already in the trunk of her car. He had just gotten worst these last few months. Roger now felt that Sheryl was depending on him to take care of everything, but that's not the case. Sheryl couldn't rest in a simple day. It seemed to her after she found out she was pregnant and had to stop working for a while, Roger changed for the worst.

Hotel Stay

Sheryl proceeded downstairs with her overnight bag. Roger asked Sheryl, "Where you are going? It's two thirty in the morning."

Sheryl replied, "What do you care? I can't rest at all; you and your friends act like I don't live here."

One of Roger friends said, "I think that we should go now."

"No!" said Roger. "It's not a problem. Sheryl, go and put the bag up and go to bed."

Sheryl told Roger no, that she was going to get a room and that she would be staying at the hotel so she could get some rest. "What money do you have?" asked Roger.

Sheryl looked at Roger with a surprised look on her face because Sheryl couldn't believe what Roger was really saying to her in front of his friends. Sheryl told Roger in a hurtful voice, "Don't worry, Roger, I do have a little money I worked for in an account. I'm not spending any of your money." Sheryl continued to the front door. She stopped, looked back, and told Roger that she couldn't do this anymore. "I can't take this abuse or neglect from you. Here's the key, I won't need them." Roger got loud with Sheryl, thinking that she was just talking out of her head. Roger yelled, "Go ahead, nobody else wants you, you're getting fat. You'll be back when you figure that out."

What You Called Me?

"Who wants a fat, pregnant woman?"

"I'm fat? You're calling me fat?" Sheryl walked back into the house yelling at Roger in front of his friends. Sheryl had had enough. She let Roger have it right in front of his friends. "Since I'm so fat, did you tell your friends what happened for me to become fat? Did you tell your friends that it's your fault that I'm pregnant? Tell your friends that you had to deceive me to get what you wanted?"

Roger's friend Jo asked Roger what Sheryl was talking about. Roger responded, "It's nothing, Jo. Could you all just call it a night, and I will talk to you all tomorrow." As Roger's friends got up from the table. Sheryl screamed with a horrifying voice, "Sit down. You all sit in my house two, sometimes three days a week; you're just as guilty as Roger. No respect for me at all because Roger said it's good. I'm pregnant right now, not by choice. It was by force to be honest, but you can sit here and disrespect me like this in front of your friends, treat me like a dog, have women in our home. What have I done to you? What have I done to get treated like this? Fifteen years now, and this is it, huh! But I tell you this; you can have your friends over every night if you want to. Roger, I will give you what you want. I'm going to get some good long, long rest."

"You said that already, Sheryl, I know that."

"I'm leaving, Roger."

"Hell, I can see that," said Roger. Sheryl grabbed her bag and walked out of the door.

CHAPTER 11

Checking In

Sheryl checked into a hotel. She got a little rest and decided to take a flight out to see her parents in California. Sheryl stayed there for two days. Roger called around, trying to find out where Sheryl was. He went to her office building. No one had spoken to her. Sheryl called no one. She had a great time with her family and decided it was time for her to go on her special ops for her job. Sheryl chose Michigan. She stayed there for two days. Sheryl had big dreams about going to Africa on her honeymoon. She knew now that it wouldn't happen any time soon; she's already made up in her mind that she would not marry Roger.

Sheryl took the flight out. It took an extra day for her to get there. She couldn't handle sitting that long, so in between flights, she booked a room to rest for a few hours to gain her composure then started fresh the next day. Sheryl finally made it to Africa. It's eight thirty in the morning. She got a cab to a hotel, got her a room, and rested for a few hours. Looking out the window was amazement for her. She decided to go to the beach for a little while. *Damn! It's very hot. I don't think that I can take a week here right now.* She went back to her room looking on the map to see what city won't be far for her to travel. She closed her eyes and said, "God, please lead me to my destiny." She ripped the map in four pieces, closed her eyes, and the one she dropped on the bed would be the country she would visit. *Oh! Jamaica. Well, Jamaica, and here I come.*

Sheryl booked a flight for the next morning. She got some rest and now was ready to fly. She checked her cell phone and saw that she has eighty-eight missed calls from Roger. She didn't return his calls, but she did call her best friend at work just to let her know that she was okay, and she didn't want Roger to know anything. Sheryl made the conversation short.

Sheryl boarded the plane. She was so tired when she sat down and got comfortable; she fell asleep. She didn't know how long she was asleep. There's only forty-five minutes left in the flight. Sheryl was very excited at the same time had little pain, but nothing major. Sheryl was not big at all; she might look about four months pregnant, but she was nearly full term. Traveling by her lonesome is not good and with no friends or family around.

In Jamaica

Sheryl had been in the city for two days now. She decided to rest and got lazy, not feeling like doing anything. So she slept and slept and slept some more. The housekeeper came in after Sheryl didn't answer the call. "Are you all right?"

"I'm just fine; I just haven't slept in weeks."

"Are you pregnant?" the housekeeper asked her.

"Yes," said Sheryl, "I'm eight months."

"Wow! You don't look it. Hell, when I was four months, I looked like I was ten months. You're doing well! So where is your husband?" asked Senate.

"Well, I'm not married."

Boyfriend asked Senate?

"Not anymore, that's why I'm here. This is where I wanted to come for my second honeymoon, but I can't even get my first one, so I decided to come now. I know it will never happen for me."

"Why do you say that? You are beautiful."

"Tell Roger that!"

"Who is Roger?"

"Someone I thought loved me, someone I've been with fifteen years. Have you checked out the scenery yet?" asked Senate.

"I don't know anything about nothing."

"Hey! I'll tell you what. I get off at five, how about I take you around? What you have in mind?"

"Well, I've always wanted to get married by the water."

"So be it, I will take you to singles' island, lots and lots of muscles."

"No, I'm not looking for a man, just a fun time."

"Oh yes, it is fun."

"I'm sorry; I didn't get your name."

"My name is Senate, and you?"

"I'm Sheryl."

"Well, nice to meet you and I will see you about six. I have to go home, shower, and change for the occasion." Sheryl took a shower, got dressed, and waited on Senate. Senate came fifteen minutes early.

Going Out

Senate knocked on the door. Sheryl opened the door to let her in. "No, no, no, no," said Senate. "What is this?" She spoke with that Jamaican accent.

"What do you mean? You're pregnant, true, but you will not look like this. Where are your clothes?"

"In the closet," said Sheryl.

"Yes, this is better." Sheryl had an evening gown that was very sexy but kind of long. Senate decided to cut it a little short. "Oh my," said Sheryl, "what are you doing?"

"You're beautiful, but now you will look beautiful and sexy. Come along, let's go."

They left the room, and Sheryl treated Senate out to dinner, and they went to the beach and boy, look at all the muscles. "Ooh, girl, you need to take me back to my room before I go into labor. I'm glad I'm pregnant! Lord, help me keep my composure. I'm getting weak at the knees. I've seen fine men, but this right here is dark and fine. Please help me sit down right here."

"Sheryl, before you sit down, will you come with me to meet my cousins and some of his friends. This is Joy, Iambi, Juju, my cousin Educed and cousin Mejia."

"Hello, how are you?" asked Educed.

"I'm doing fine," responded Sheryl.

"Well, I just brought her over to meet you all, we have to go now."

"Hey," said Mejia. "Hey, hook me up with her."

"No, Mejia, she just got out of a bad relationship."

"I just want to take her out," said Mejia.

"With your friends?" said Senate. "I don't think so, get lost." Senate's cousin was not a good friend to anyone; she tried to avoid him at all cost. She let Sheryl know not to hold any conversation with him or anyone that wore scarves.

The sun was setting, and Sheryl said she would like to lie on the beach to watch the sunset. Senate said fine and lay beside Sheryl on a towel. "I can't stay long, my friend will be home in a couple of hour and I didn't cook yet."

"Well, go then."

"I won't leave you alone out here."

"Should I be afraid of anything?"

"No, it's not like that. It's just like any place. But you are pregnant."

"I'll be fine." Sheryl was only going to stay for thirty minutes. She watched the sunset as the sun was closing. She began to close her eyes with it, not knowing she would actually fall asleep, and she did. Sheryl was actually sleeping for about an hour. Sleeping and being as still as she was.

CHAPTER 12

The Scare

A man named Jayson walked past slowly. Sheryl didn't move. Jayson called out to her and said, "Madam!" There still no movement. Jayson then bent down and touched her throat to see if she was breathing. Sheryl screamed. "I'm sorry, I'm not going to hurt you," Jayson assured her. "You are alone out here. Why?" Sheryl was now holding her stomach and her chest. "Please sit down, madam. You are pregnant, yes!" Sheryl nodded her head; she didn't have enough strength to talk. She's stepping back from Jayson. "I will not hurt you." He pulled out his card to show Sheryl that he secured the beach at night that's why he's there. "I promise I will not hurt you. Here! You need to sit down. Are you having pain?"

Sheryl said, "Just a little."

"I'm so sorry I've frightened you, please forgive me."

"It's okay! I just fell asleep with the sunset, I didn't mean to. Well, I have to go now."

"Well, I can walk you home?"

"I don't live here, I have a room."

"Well, can I walk you to your room?"

"No! Thanks. That won't be necessary." She took a couple of steps and saw a couple of guys with scarves on; she looked back and told Jayson, "Well, can you walk with me?" Jayson started to walk with Sheryl. "No funny business," said Sheryl.

"You don't have to worry about me; I know how to respect a lady." Sheryl smiled and began to walk with Jayson.

Pain hit her viciously out of nowhere. She buckled to one knee; Jayson grabbed her. "Please not now," said Jayson.

"I'm okay, it's just normal contraction."

"Contractions, how far along are you?"

"I'm thirty-seven weeks."

"Where are you from?"

"I am from the States!"

"You're so far from home. Where's your husband, your family?"

"I'm alone here."

"What made you do something like that? You know you really need to leave now, go back to America. They will not let you leave the city after Saturday."

"Why is that?" Sheryl asked.

"When women here are thirty-eight weeks, no travelling time given, so please go or call your family."

Sheryl looked at her cell phone. She saw more missed calls from Roger, and at the same time, she could hear his voice cursing her. She visualized the pain and disrespect Roger put her through; she looked at Jayson and said to him, "I have no one."

Jayson looked at Sheryl. "That can't be true."

"Well, it is," said Sheryl. "A man is not a good friend to me right now."

"I take it you've been hurt?" asked Jayson.

Tears came down Sheryl's face. "Yes, fifteen years wasted on one man, for what?"

"Well, you with child?" asked Jayson.

"Yes, I'm with child he deceived me to have. He set me up, nothing planned. I don't regret the child, just the man."

Sheryl's not letting Jayson know that she's in pain, but he knew from the expression on her face. "You are in labor, the baby is ready."

"You think so?" asked Sheryl.

"Yes, please, come now."

"Well, it doesn't hurt that bad and it always goes away."

Jayson looked at Sheryl and said, "I'm not sure, and neither are you. Let's just go to the hospital. See what the doctor has to say."

"Just let me sit at this table for a few minutes. If it continues, I will go, I promise."

"Okay," said Jayson. "Five minutes then we go to the hospital." Sheryl and Jayson sat at the table and continued to talk. The pain eased up a little as Sheryl repositioned herself.

Jayson began asking a lot of question that Sheryl didn't really want to answer; she answered some but decided she would like to lie on the beach for a few more minutes. Jayson, with no obligation at home or nothing to do at that time, agreed to take her back near the water. He unfolded her towel onto the ground and helped Sheryl down slowly.

Jayson stood there, having a conversation with Sheryl. Sheryl looked up and thanked Jayson for helping her and not trying anything funny with her. He smiled and said to Sheryl, "I do have a mother too. I wouldn't want anyone to take advantage of her or my sisters. Besides, you are pregnant."

"What is that suppose to mean?" asked Sheryl.

"Don't get defensive. I'm only saying that here, we don't put any stress on our wives or girlfriend when they're pregnant. We give more help to them."

The Gang

Jayson saw a crowd coming from a distance, but as he continued to talk to Sheryl, he realized who the group was. He told Sheryl to close her eyes and relax. He didn't want to scare her by telling her who was approaching them. He sat on the towel next to Sheryl; Jayson got pretty close. Sheryl said, "Watch it now. I'm not trying anything; I just want you to remain calm. We have company, honey!"

"Honey." said Sheryl.

"Just calm down, you will understand. Just follow my lead, okay?"

"Okay," responded Sheryl.

The groups of guys were now where Sheryl and Jayson were.

"What's up, Jayson?" said one of the guys out of the group.

"What's going on?" asked Jayson.

"Who is this fine thing you have here?"

"This is my friend Sheryl."

While dragging out the words, one of the guys said, "Well hello, Sheryl." Sheryl didn't speak at all. She was then ready to leave, but she didn't move as Jayson asked her not to.

Jayson asked the guys, "What I can do for you?"

"Well, nothing," responded the group.

"Well, my lady and I came out to spend some time together, so if you don't mind."

"Sure thing no problem!" The group walked off, and Jayson watched them as they left the beach.

Jayson looked at Sheryl and said, "Five more minutes then I'm taking you home."

"Why?" asked Sheryl.

"Because that's a gang, and all men are not good here."

"Well, it is getting late," said Sheryl. "I think we better go now."

"Are you sure?" said Jayson. "I'm willing to give you a few more minutes."

"That's okay," said Sheryl, "there's always tomorrow."

"So would you like for me to come with you?" asked Jayson.

"Sure, why not? You're the only one I feel real comfortable with right now."

"Just right now Jayson asked. "I'm just joking. Come on, Sheryl, let me help you up. I don't want you to hurt yourself."

"It's two of us," said Sheryl. "Well, I think I can manage that answer, Jayson."

Jayson let Sheryl know that he was going to lift her up by putting both of his hands around her waist. He told Sheryl to turn onto her side and lean up slightly so he could raise her from the left side. "Wow!" said Sheryl. "That was the easiest I've ever gotten up. Thank you so much."

"You're very welcome. Come along, I'll drive you home.

Walking with Pain

Sheryl and Jayson began to walk. They made it about a half of a block, with a hum in Sheryl's voice. Jayson immediately asked her, "Are you all right?"

"Whoa," said Sheryl, "this pain is umm. Ooh!"

"Here, let me help you. My car is around the corner. Do you think you can make it there?"

"I made it this far. It hurt like hell, but I'll make it."

"Are you sure?"

"You know you can call a cab. I don't want to mess up your car."

This car is just material things, which can be cleaned or replaced! Here we are." Jayson pushed the button on his key chain and opened the door for Sheryl.

She again asked Jayson, "Are you sure? What if my water breaks? Then you have to clean the car."

Jayson looked at Sheryl with a smile and said, "You worry too much!"

"You are driving me to the hospital in a beamer?"

"Yes, I am. I drive one of the best." Jayson sped off into traffic.

"You don't have to rush," said Sheryl. "It's probably early contractions, and I'm not due yet."

"Well, we are going just to make sure."

The hospital was now five minutes away. They continued to talk. Sheryl asked a few questions of her own. "What do you do?"

Jayson responded, "I sell real state, and I have a law firm downtown."

"Wow," said Sheryl while grunting. "So you're a lawyer?"

"Yes, one of the best," answered Jayson.

"Whoa, okay, it's getting harder," Sheryl said with more grunting and moaning.

"Are you okay?" asked Jayson.

"Yes, but it's starting to hurt like hell."

"Please tell me if you feel like you can't go on."

"It's okay, I can make it, I promise." Jayson reached over and touched Sheryl's stomach. With all the pain she's having, it felt pretty good to her. So Jayson started rubbing her stomach in a circular motion. Sheryl asked Jayson, "Are you sure you don't have kids"

"I'm positive I don't. I have sisters and a good mother who trained me very well how to treat a lady and to make her feel comfortable."

"Well," said Sheryl, "you're doing a great job."

CHAPTER 13

Blue Lights

Just around the corner from the hospital, with Jayson speeding, a police turned his blue lights on and stopped Jayson. "Sir, you are speeding in the town zone. What's the reason?" He sat back and looked at Sheryl who was all moaning and groaning. "Is she in labor?" the officer asked Jayson.

"Yes, she is." The officer immediately called the hospital that a patient was on the way and that he would be escorting them there. It didn't take a minute and Sheryl was now at the hospital. The doctors met her at the door and started checking her pulse, pressure temperature. Her stats were good. They were taking her in the room and wanted Jayson to stay to answer some questions about her pregnancy. The only thing that Jayson could tell them was that she was not due for almost two more weeks. They went into the room and asked Jayson to come along with them just in case he had to make any decision. He was trying to tell them that he's of no relation to Sheryl, but they would always cut him off from talking. So he played along with them because Sheryl didn't have any one there at all and she only trusted him. Jayson didn't want to be responsible for anything that might have happened. Sheryl was stable, and they were prepping her to have her baby. She talked to Jayson, thanking him for all he had done for her.

"You can go home and get some rest, you have a family too."

Jayson called his mother and told her what's going on. She knew now that Jayson won't be home tonight, when he told Sheryl that he was staying with her. "What?" said Sheryl? "Why aren't you going home?"

"I will be here until everything is over and you are safe in your apartment or on a plane back to the States."

"No!" said Sheryl. "I'm not ready to go back there."

"What is so bad?" asked Jayson. "Don't answer that. Just focus on the baby, we will talk later."

"Could you keep my purse and my towel please, well, I trust you," said Sheryl. Jayson smiled and walked off. He sat in the waiting room for about fifteen minutes, then the nurse ran, calling, "Jayson, Jayson! Are you Jayson?"

"Yes, I am. Sheryl is asking for you, she said she wants you there."

"Me?" asked Jayson.

"Yes, aren't you the father?"

"Well," said Jayson.

"Sir, we don't have time to talk, it's almost time. Come along with me."

Don't Leave Me

Jayson immediately ran behind the nurse. Jayson made it to the room and whispered to Sheryl, "You want me in here while you have your son?"

"Yes, I do?" answered Sheryl. "I'm lonely in here, I have no one else." Sheryl started to cry.

Jayson gave her a hug and said, "Don't cry. I'm here. I won't leave you. I'll be here as long as you need me, I promised."

Sheryl shouted once in a big scream. "Oh my god, this shit really hurts!" She held Jayson's hands, and he patted her forehead with a wet cloth.

"You're doing good, sweetheart. Just listen to the doctors." Jayson was trying not to look below Sheryl's gown, but it's hard not to, considering he's never experienced a birth before and he wanted to know what was taking place between Sheryl's legs. "Jesus," stated Jayson.

"What is it?" asked Sheryl.

"Nothing bad, it's just that your bottom is growing right before my very eyes."

"Oh, Jayson," said the doctor, "it's a part of expansion that has to take place for the baby to come out, it will shrink back to the regular size."

"Oh! Okay, whoa! I thought the baby was killing her." The nurse laughed, patted Jayson on the back, and told him just keep her comfortable.

Sheryl was in labor for three hours after she was admitted. She had a beautiful baby boy. She didn't have a name for him yet. She asked Jayson his whole name, and he told Sheryl that his full name was Jayson Montero Colbert. "I like it," said Sheryl.

"You like what?" asked Jayson.

"Your name I want to name my son after something good that I will always remember."

"May I ask what that is?" asked Jayson.

"If you don't mind, I would like to name my son Jayson Montero, but I will call him Montero."

Jayson laughed and said to Sheryl, "Name your son after the father, it's traditional."

"Not where I'm from," said Sheryl.

"Well, if you would like to do that, it's okay with me, as long as I'm the godfather."

"Of course!" said Sheryl. She was hurting so bad she only wanted good things for her and Roger, but she had no strong love for him like she used to.

Jayson consoled Sheryl for an hour; she finally dosed off and went to sleep. Jayson told the nurse that he would be back; he wanted to take a shower and freshen up. "Don't you want to hold your baby?" asked the nurse. "Well, come hold your son before you go. You know a baby never forgets a parent's scent."

"Well okay, just five minutes. I just wanted to be back before she wakes up." Jayson held the baby for fifteen minutes; he hugged and kissed him, just loving him like a father should. Jayson went to see his mom and told her what happened and that he thought that Sheryl was the one for him.

His mother said, "Be careful! You waited all these years, just be careful, son."

"I will," replied Jayson.

"Do you want something to eat before you leave?" asked Trisha, his mother.

"No," Jayson responded, "I will get something on the way. I want to get back before Sheryl wakes up." Jayson was now on his way back to the hospital. Sheryl was still asleep. Jayson stopped by the florist and picked up a teddy bear and some balloons. He filled up Sheryl's room with flowers and balloons until the nurse had to stop more from coming in. Jayson sat in the chair next to Sheryl's bed, holding Montero. There's a little movement in Sheryl. She's awakened.

"Hello, why are you still here? You don't have to sit here and babysit me, you've helped me enough, don't you think?"

"I went home to take a shower. Now I'm here to make sure that you're all right."

"Look, I'm just fine. Since I've been here, you have helped me, cared for me, and that bothers me because—"

"No! No!" Jayson interrupted her. "Not right now. I want you to focus on you and your son right now, that's it."

"But,"-said Sheryl.

"No buts. Here, hold your son. Be happy, I'm happy for you."

"I'm sorry," said Sheryl.

"No need to feel bad, everything's going to be fine."

"Where are you staying?"

"I'm in Shoed hotel on Sixth, why?"

"You can come to my house."

"No!" said Sheryl, "I will not impose on you."

"You're not imposing on me, I insist, just until you're better."

"Why are you doing this, you don't know me. I'm a stranger in your town. Do you take everyone in you meet?"

"No funny stuff. We will be in separate rooms like roommates."

"Roommates," said Sheryl. "What about your mother?"

"I don't live with my mother, I live alone."

"Yeah Okay, a very handsome guy like yourself doesn't have a woman, and you live alone?"

"Yes, why is it so hard to believe with a smile?"

"Well, that's just one in a million. You have some good men in this world, yes, but why . . ." Sheryl immediately stopped talking. "Okay, I will stay for a few days, and then I will find a place of my own."

"Wait a minute," said Jayson. "Why would you find a place here? You have no family and you're just visiting, right?"

"Well, maybe I need to stay a while to clear my head."

"Okay, just let me know if there is anyone you want me to call."

"No," said Sheryl, "don't."

"Well, your phone has been ringing off the hook with calls. I didn't answer; I didn't want to invade your privacy."

"I have no privacy," said Sheryl, "but it's okay. I'll check the calls tomorrow."

"Sheryl, I will have someone pick up your things in the morning from the hotel, I will need your keys."

"Look in my purse."

"Well, it's in my car. I will go get it, I won't stay long. Let me hold Montero for a minute then I want you to get some rest, and I will see you first thing in the morning."

"No! Please don't leave me here."

"I want you to rest." said Jayson.

"Please! I don't know anyone."

"Okay, let me step out and make a couple of calls and have someone to come by to get the key and I'll be back up."

"Okay," said Sheryl. Sheryl turned on the TV while Jayson was downstairs waiting on his butler to come get the key to get Sheryl's things from the hotel.

CHAPTER 14

Roger Calls

Jayson went back in the hospital when Sheryl's phone rang. Jayson debated whether to answer the phone or not. He didn't answer. Jayson realized that this was the same number that called fifty-eight times that same night. He decided to answer as he walked toward the elevator. "Hello," said Jayson.

"Who in the hell is this?" asked Roger. "This is Jayson, and you?"

"Where is Sheryl?" Immediately Jayson kind of figured that it was the guy Sheryl was running away from.

"Well, the person that owns this phone is not here."

"Well, where she is?" asked Roger. "Sir, this phone was left in the restaurant. Someone turned it in just a couple of hours ago."

"What restaurant is that?" asked Roger. Jayson hung up; he didn't want to make things bad for Sheryl if he answered any questions. He didn't want to worry Sheryl about the call, so he waited until she was released and comfortable in his home.

Sheryl was released late that afternoon. Jayson's limo picked Sheryl and the baby up from the hospital. He had everything that Sheryl needed for the baby, including a nanny at the house who had already decorated an extra bedroom near his room upstairs. Jayson went up to Sheryl's room where she awaited for her discharge papers to be signed. Jayson had to sign the paper, letting the hospital know that she had somewhere suitable to go. The nurses at the station knew exactly who he was. Of course, all the ladies started whispering to each other, "Boy, he is fine. I've never seen her before. How did she get him?"

Sheryl heard what they were saying, and she said to them, "He's just a good friend. Do you want me to deliver a message for you?"

"Will you?" Candy wrote her number quickly on a piece of paper and handed it to Sheryl. "Tell him call me."

"Okay, I will." Sheryl stuck the piece of paper underneath the baby blanket. Here came Jayson.

"Are you ready?"

"Yes, I am." Jayson pushed Sheryl and the baby out in front of the hospital then a limo pulled up. The driver got out, came to Sheryl, and headed for the baby.

"No! Get away from me."

"Sheryl, Sheryl, it's my driver, baby, he won't hurt you."

"Your driver Sheryl asked?"

"Yes."

"What do you have a driver for?"

"I didn't feel like driving, and the beamer is too small to bring the baby in. We will talk later."

Sheryl was on her way to something she could never imagine. Jayson's home was about twenty minutes from the hospital. "Wow," said Sheryl, "this must be the rich part of the country."

"Well, some are just wealthy. Besides, it's not that expensive."

"What do you call not expensive?" asked Sheryl.

"In your country, how much would that house cost, you think?" Sheryl said about three hundred and fifty thousand dollars. "Wow," said Jayson. "Here, this house is about one hundred and thirty-five."

"Why so cheap?" asked Sheryl.

"In this country, there's no insurance coverage, so everybody's basically at risk and basically on their own, so they make it affordable. The land is high, but the home dirt cheap."

Jayson's Home

The driver turned into the driveway, but Sheryl saw nothing. As the driver drove, lights lit up. Sheryl saw a tall rising she thought was an office building. The tint was dark; she couldn't see anything. Now the driver had circled the driveway. When he stopped the car and proceeded to open Sheryl's door, all the security lights came on. "Oh my god, you live here?"

"Yes, this is my home."

"You live alone in this? I can't do this, it's huge."

"That's why I have security." Four guys ran up on Sheryl.

Jayson said, "She's fine, she's with me. She's my guest and she's free to mingle." Jayson's security went back to their post while Jayson grabbed the carriage for Sheryl. The nanny came with the wheelchair for Sheryl to sit on.

"No!" said Sheryl. "I want to walk in on my own."

Jayson said no. "Sit, Sheryl, it'll be fine!"

"No, I just want to take my time and walk in."

"Okay," said Jayson, "but wait just a moment." Jayson handed the nanny the baby and told her to take him upstairs.

He took Sheryl's hand and put his arm around her waist and walked with her into the house. Sheryl walked in the front door and wiped her forehead. "I need something to drink!" All Sheryl saw was marble floors, waterfalls, aquariums, lights, and housekeepers. She made it as far as the living room. Being kind of sore, she couldn't walk anymore. It would have taken her ten minutes to get upstairs; this house had the total of thirty rooms in it.

Jayson sat Sheryl down in front of the fireplace and brought her a glass of lemonade. "Jayson, I can't impose on you like this, it's best if I leave tomorrow."

"Nonsense," said Jayson, "you will stay here as long as you want. Do you need me to help you with anything? Yes?"

"Before I get comfortable, help me to my room so I can put on something more comfortable." Jayson helped Sheryl upstairs to his master's suite. "Jayson, this is your room? No, I couldn't," said Sheryl.

"Yes," said Jayson, "it's yours now."

"No! I can't do that, all the rooms I'm sure are beautiful. The baby and I can stay in a smaller room."

"No," said Jayson, "the baby has his own room, and this is yours."

"You gave my son his own room? He's too young."

"He has a nanny twenty-four hours a day, and I want what's best for you and Montero. For the next few days, you will need your rest as well as he does." Sheryl again stressed how much she thanked Jayson for helping her and her son.

Jayson said to himself, *you are helping me. I know you are the one for me, and that little boy will be my son. He will have my last name.*

Jayson constantly made sure that Sheryl was comfortable with her stay and made sure that the housekeepers did their job. It didn't matter what Sheryl wanted, it was there without hesitation.

Help Me Undress

Sheryl tried to take off her clothes, but she was very sore. The nanny heard her and went in to help her. But Sheryl refused to let the nanny help her. Jayson went into the room and caught Sheryl with her pants down. "Oh!" said Sheryl.

"I'm sorry," said Jayson as he walked back out of the room.

"It's okay, just don't look, but pull this off slowly for me and close your eyes."

Jayson walked with his eyes close as Sheryl stepped back as Jayson got closer to her. She's playing with him. He heard her voice but seemed to be touching the bed. "Sheryl, where are you?"

"I'm over here, I'm hurting, and I'm moving faster than you."

He laughed, "Oh! Okay, so this is funny." He opened his eyes, and Sheryl was sitting on the bed with the baby. "There you are. I like your sense of humor, and it's great," said Jayson.

"I haven't had fun in a while," said Sheryl. "I just needed to laugh."

"That's a good thing, everyone should be happy," responded Jayson. "Well, I will be going to get some rest myself. I have to go to work in the morning. Well, not physically working, but I have to go into the office for a couple of hours."

"Okay, get some rest, we'll be just fine." As Jayson started to walk off, he double-backed and kissed little Montero on the forehead, and he looked into Sheryl's eyes. They stared at each other for a moment.

Jayson said to Sheryl, "You have some beautiful eyes." And he kissed her on both sides of her cheek. He said good night.

As he walked toward the door, Sheryl called him, "Jayson."

"Yes, Sheryl."

"You know this room is big enough for two beds, you know."

"Sheryl, you're not afraid to sleep alone here, are you? No one will come in here; you can lock your door."

"No! I'm not afraid." Jayson didn't question her again; he just padded the floor beside the bed and slept there. Sheryl kept looking on the floor throughout the night to make sure that Jayson was still there.

It's about three in the morning and Jayson had to use the bathroom. He wasn't on the floor when Sheryl looked. She panicked! "Jayson!" with a loud scream, she called him three times before he came in.

He whispered, "What is it, Sheryl?"

"Where is the baby?"

"I just fed him and put him back to sleep. He's fine, he's resting, and the nanny is right there with him."

"Why didn't you answer me when I called you?"

"I was holding him and didn't want to yell. I would have woken him up. Can we talk because something is really bothering you and I want to know what it is? I need to know what you are really running from. Is it Roger?"

"How do you know about Roger?"

"Well, he called the phone last night at the hospital."

"You didn't tell me that," said Sheryl. "Look, I don't have any secrets, and I'm not a liar. But I told him one last night to protect you because I didn't know and don't know what is going on."

"What did he say?"

"He asked who I was, I told him my name. I asked him his, he wouldn't tell me, he just asked for you, and then he asked me what I was doing with your phone. I told him that I didn't know to whom phone was. That it was left in a restaurant. I hung up because he kept asking things that I didn't have an answer for, and that was it. Now tell me what's going on."

Sheryl began to cry. "Fifteen years . . . I gave him. We were together for a long time. I never thought in a million years that I would be talking to another man about this. Roger and I agreed not to have children for the first four years of our career or after we were married, and he decided he wanted a child sooner, so he took it upon himself to play God with my contraceptive and I got pregnant. And believe it or not, I just found out two and a half months ago."

Jayson responded, "You didn't find out for almost five months? Sheryl, tell me what is going on with you? Why are you so afraid of him?"

"He started getting physical with me a few of months ago. He lost respect for me; I don't know what I did to deserve that. I have no friends because of him. He calls me fat, a bitch, just whatever comes to mind at the time. He and his friends play cards late at night at the house, drink and bring women into our home while I'm trying to sleep. A couple of times I had to get a room just to get some rest. I couldn't take it anymore. When I left after two that morning, he knew I was going to get a room, but he didn't know that I wasn't coming back. I haven't been back since. I don't want to go back, and I remember some months back he told me that he will kill me before he let someone else have me. I really don't want to put you and your family in danger. We really need to be going before he finds out that I had the baby and living with a man."

"No!" Jayson said. "You are not going anywhere. If you are happy here, then this is where you will be. We will talk about this tomorrow."

"Hey!" said Sheryl. "Could you just lie here for tonight please?"

"Are you sure?" Jayson asked.

"Yes, it will be fine," said Sheryl.

"Okay!" said Jayson. "I will sleep on this side if it makes you feel better."

"Thank you so much."

CHAPTER 15

The Dream

Sheryl fell asleep within twenty to thirty minutes. Jayson watched her sleep, and then he finally dosed off. Sheryl started moving violently in her sleeps as if she was trying to get away from something. Jayson called out to Sheryl, "Wake up; it's just a dream, everything's all right." Sheryl rolled over and lay closer to Jayson.

"No funny business, I just need to know that you are here." Sheryl was now sound asleep; she slept through the night. She didn't even know Jayson had already left and it's already one o'clock in the evening. Sheryl got up, checked on the baby, went in the bathroom, and took a shower. After a nice, warm shower, she went downstairs to take a closer look at Jayson's home. *Wow! This is so gorgeous.*

While Jayson was thinking how to get Sheryl to stay here with him, Roger's at home plotting how to find Sheryl and bring her back home. He had no knowledge of Sheryl having the baby. But he's called around trying to ask everyone that Sheryl knew, including her parents, but they won't tell Roger a thing. It's been two months.

Sheryl was still living with Jayson. They became very close but never got to the point of intimacy, and Jayson never pressured her or made any advances toward Sheryl. Sheryl finally got up the nerve to call Roger, telling him that she wouldn't be coming back and that she's leaving him. She told Roger that she would be coming soon to pack her things. Roger played dumb, like nothing ever happened. "What are you talking about?" Roger asked Sheryl.

"Do you even have to ask?" said Sheryl. "I was nothing to you when I was there. You did what you wanted when you wanted. I just can't take any more of the disrespect."

Moving On

"I'm moving on with my life."

"What about my son? You can't just leave and take my son."

"You can see your son, but you won't be seeing me, it's over," said Sheryl.

"What do you mean it's over?" replied Roger.

"I won't be moving back to the States. Montero is now two months old, and we are doing just fine," said Sheryl.

"Where are you?" asked Roger.

"Look, I want my son to have you, his father, in his life, but I don't want this relationship. I'll talk to you later."

Before Sheryl hung up, Roger yelled, "I will see you in court!" Roger called Sheryl phone back, but Sheryl refused to answer. He finally left a message on Sheryl's phone, "You will not leave me and take my son. I love you. It will never be over, never. I will never let you go never.

Sheryl checked the voicemail and listened to the message Roger left on her phone. She knew that no one around her would be safe, so she decided to pack up the few things she had, the baby, and left Jayson's home; but Jayson pulled up with flowers in his hands. He walked in and saw the luggage; he went upstairs to Sheryl and asked her what was going on. "I have to go; I can't have you in my affairs or your family in danger."

"What are you talking about Sheryl?"

"I called Roger just to let him know that I will be coming to get my things and that I was leaving, and he didn't take it lightly. He told me that he won't let me go." Sheryl dialed her voicemail and put it on speakerphone so Jayson could hear what Roger left on her voicemail. While they were listening to the voicemail, Roger left another voicemail telling Sheryl that he would kill the man that she was with and that she would never be safe. "I will find you and kill you. You will never be safe. I will find you." Jayson hung up the phone and immediately called the police and made a report. Jayson was well known in his country. There's nothing that no one wouldn't do for him. Being that, Sheryl had been in Jamaica for more than a month and bore a child there. Montero was considered to be a resident. The police took a report and let Sheryl know that Roger would be arrested if he's caught on the property.

Sheryl was scared and frightened, but she didn't want any trouble in Jayson's home, so she called a cab and asked the cabdriver to take her to a hotel. When the cabdriver came, Jayson turned him away. Sheryl waited for the cab; she knew that the cab should have been there by now. She called the cab company, and the operator told Sheryl that her cab was cancelled. She immediately walked downstairs, calling Jayson. "Did you cancel my car?"

"Yes, I did. I will not let you go out there with my son."

"What?" said Sheryl?

"I'm sorry, but he's like my son. I care for you both. Please unpack your things. Sheryl, have I ever harmed you or made you felt uncomfortable? Do you trust me?"

"Yes," Sheryl said. "I do trust you? But I also care enough for you to leave your home."

"Nonsense," said Jayson, "you're staying here, end of conversation. Now please don't frighten the child. Get dressed; I'll take you both out to eat."

"Are you sure?" asked Sheryl.

"If I didn't care for you or didn't want you here, I would have let you go a long time ago."

"Well, I do thank you again for all you've done, but if I'm going to be staying here, I need to let my landlord know and turn in my keys."

"Okay, I will take you tomorrow afternoon," said Jayson.

"That's okay. I will let the nanny keep Montero until I get back. It won't take long."

"Are you sure?" asked Jayson.

"Yes, I'll be just fine. Besides, it'll give me a little time out to myself. That'll be good I guess."

"Be careful, and don't mingle!"

"Believe me, I know." Jayson allowed Sheryl to use his beamer. His driver took him to the office. Sheryl let the nanny know that she's leaving and that she would be back in a couple of hours.

CHAPTER 16

The Hotel Room

Sheryl didn't know that Roger was there and had been staying at the same hotel for the last two days. Sheryl continued on to her room to pick up the rest of her things; she found her room fully demolished, torn to pieces. She was stepping over broken glass and found that everything she left was burnt. She continued into the second room where she had set up for the baby, but they never returned to the room after the birth of her baby. Sheryl went down the hall. When she turned the corner, she was grabbed from behind. Lo and behold, it's Roger! "You think you're safe? Where are you staying?" Roger was screaming. "I tracked this room down a few days ago, but no one knows you here, you can't get any information because the people won't talk, but that's just fine. I have you now, I told you, if I can't have you, no one will. Where's my son?"

"He's in daycare," answered Sheryl.

"I want to see my son."

"No!" said Sheryl. "I don't want this in my life that's why I left." He punched Sheryl in her face. She tried to defend herself, hitting Roger with a lamp that was on the desk. Roger then continued to hit Sheryl as if they were in a boxing match. He punched Sheryl down on the floor, kicking her in her back, stomach, and in her head. Sheryl was bleeding from everywhere as he beat her. He continued to talk to her, trying to find out where she was staying. Sheryl refused to tell him to protect Jayson and his family. No matter how hard Roger hit her, she refused to tell him anything. All Sheryl could do was cry. The more she cried, the more her face started burning.

She's now gasping for air. Roger held his hands up, ready to strike Sheryl again. A knock at the door Roger paused. "Housekeeping" Roger quickly dragged Sheryl in the hall. She was not responding at the time. Roger went to the door, and the house keeper told him that she needed to get in. He was trying to talk the housekeeper into letting him stay for another day. Roger offered to pay the housekeeper right at the door, but the house keeper told Roger that he would have to go up front to the office to get another room because that room had been already booked for the next two weeks. He refused to go to the front office. Sheryl moved her leg against the wall.

The housekeeper heard the grunting sound and asked Roger who was in the room. Roger said, "Fine, give me a minute, I'll be right out." The housekeeper never had seen Roger before and didn't feel comfortable about how he was acting. The housekeeper Senate looked at the room number and asked where Sheryl was? Roger didn't answer her, so she called for security. Roger immediately pulled the housekeeper in and hit her across the head twice.

The housekeeper didn't give the front desk the room number she was actually inquiring about, so they had to look for the room. The security got to the fourth room to where Sheryl and the housekeeper were. When they opened the door, the housekeeper was just getting up, holding the side of her head. The security asked her what happened. The housekeeper told security that she didn't know what was going on, that she remembered talking to the man then she got hit. She knew that the man who hit her was hiding something; the housekeeper heard that noise again. She then walked down the hall, and when she turned the corner, she screamed immediately, "Get an ambulance! Call 911. Oh my god, is that you, Sheryl? Yes, it is.

"Who was that man?" asked the security.

"I don't know," said the housekeeper. "I've never seen him before. Who would do something like this?"

Calling Jayson

The security guard asked, "Does she have any family or someone that we need to call?" No one knew Sheryl but the housekeeper Senate. "Here, this is her cell phone. Well, let's check her cell phone, maybe we can get some information about her." The security guard then grabbed Sheryl's cell phone from the housekeeper and browsed through Sheryl's phone and realizes that she's not from there. All of the numbers in Sheryl's phone were not familiar to him. Only two numbers were local, which the officer knew were the hotel she was staying prior to having her baby and Jayson's business number. They tried Jayson's number first. They got no answer because he was in a meeting.

They proceeded to prep Sheryl for the ambulance and took her down to the town hospital. It wasn't ten minutes after the security made the call that Jayson returned the call. The first thing the security guard asked Jayson was, "What relation is Sheryl to him?" Jayson proceeded to tell the guard that Sheryl was a guest of his in his home and they became very close.

"Why do you ask?" said Jayson.

"I'm sorry to tell you."

Jayson screamed, "Tell me what? No! No! No!" Jayson dropped the phone on his desk, fearing what the officer was about to tell him.

"Sir, sir," the officer was calling out for Jayson.

"What is it?"

"Sheryl has been beaten pretty badly, and she's at the town hospital."

"What?" said Jayson? "Who would do such a thing? Do you even have a clue?"

The guard asked Jayson "Is there any family members that needed to be called?" Jayson told him no, that he's the only family she had. "

Where's my son?"

"I don't know anything about a kid. Are you sure there's a kid?"

"Yes, I'm sure; she has been living with me for a few months now."

"Let me call the station and let them know about the child, and we will keep you posted."

"Thanks!" Jayson hung up the phone and called the nanny. She didn't pick up on the first call Jayson made. He redialed the number. Now he's worried and shaking at the same time. Phone rang twice, and the nanny picked up. "This is Jayson, do you have Montero?"

"Well yes, sir, he's asleep right now. Is there something wrong?"

Tears began to pour down Jayson's face. "I'll talk to you when I get home. Just lock the doors, and let no one that you don't know in. Everything will be fine. Is the security still out there?"

"Yes," said the nanny.

"Okay, tell them stay overtime until I tell them different. I will call you in an hour or so." Jayson rushed down to the hospital to see Sheryl. The doctors wouldn't allow him into the room until he agreed to talk to them first so they could really let him know what was going on and what he would be looking at when he went into the room.

Comatose

They proceeded to tell Jayson that Sheryl was in a coma and it's indefinite when she would come out of it. Until the swelling went down, they couldn't give any diagnosis. They also let Jayson know that her face was really messed up and that he had to be really strong when he went in there. They offered Jayson some support from a church group, but he refused. Jayson was now ready to go see Sheryl. He walked in her room slowly; he turned his head slightly to the left so he wouldn't see her directly. But he couldn't help it. He walked straight to Sheryl's bed and fell to his knees and cried like a baby. The nurse came in, but he didn't want to be bothered at the time. He shouted, "Go, go." He grabbed Sheryl's hands. "Baby who did this to you? Who did this? Oh my god, baby I know that I should have taken you myself. Please be all right!" Jayson sobbed for an half an hour. He refused to leave Sheryl's bedside. But he had to go check on Montero. No matter what Jayson had to do, he always put Sheryl first. He took some time off from the office to stay by Sheryl's side; he didn't know when she would awake and he wanted to be there.

Roger still in the area; he tried to see Sheryl in the hospital, but he couldn't get through security. You had to be family. No one knew who or what Roger was to Sheryl, but he let them know that he was her kid's father. They didn't know at the time that Roger had done this to Sheryl, so Roger was not in question. Jayson had no knowledge of Roger being at the hospital. As he came walking back from the soda machine, he saw a man standing in Sheryl's room. Jayson immediately went in and asked, "Who are you? What are you doing in here?"

Roger responded, "I am family."

"Oh yeah!" said Jayson. "What is your name? Show me some identification." Immediately Roger took off down the hall, and Jayson called for security. No one could enter Sheryl's room without going through Jayson. Jayson told the security guard that it might be a possibility that was the person who had done this.

They kept a close eye on Sheryl's room. Everyone must have a badge on or they won't be allowed in Sheryl's room. Jayson had to leave the hospital from time to time to check on Montero, who's now four and a half months old! Jayson constantly took Montero to see his mother in the hospital even though she's in a coma. A child could sense that motherly love.

Sometimes Jayson would read a book to Montero and Sheryl as she lay there with no movement. Jayson never doubted or lost hope when it came down to Sheryl. He would sometimes ask the doctor if there were any changes in Sheryl at this point. The doctor would tell Jayson no. There are no changes for good or bad, she's just sleeping.

CHAPTER 17

CT scan

"We will be doing a CT scan in a couple of days. What we want to do is a little plastic surgery to her face to correct those scars. But we won't do that until she awakes. I just really hate for her to see herself in this way, but there's nothing we can do at this point. Let's just hope for the best, okay?"

"Thank you, Doctor."

Montero started calling for his mother, but there was no response from Sheryl. He then held out both of his arms, reaching for his mother.

"Ma, Ma," he kept calling her and started to cry. Jayson's heart had gotten full; he started to tear up, calling Montero's name, "It'll be all right, baby. Mommy is sick right now." He kissed Sheryl on her forehead and said, "I'll be back as soon as I can." He left the hospital with Montero to take him back to the nanny. It was very hurtful for Jayson to see Montero cry like that. Jayson always made sure that he's there to tuck Montero in at night. He didn't want to miss a day of that. When you think the worst have been done, what more can someone lay on you?

Sheryl's Disorderly Discharged

The hospital called while Jayson was putting Montero to bed. "We are very sorry, but there is nothing we can do at this point for Sheryl. Her insurance company just e-mailed us confirming they will not cover her stay at the hospital, and we have exhausted the charity box. If we don't have any source of payment by the end of the week, we will have to release her from the hospital."

"What are you talking about?" asked Jayson. "You are worrying about money instead of her health. This woman is lying in your hospital bed fighting for her life, and you call me about money. Are you serious right now?"

"I'm sorry, Jayson, but it's out of my hands. There's nothing that I can do at this point."

"You don't touch her. I will make other arrangements for her, you need not to worry about the cost, and I got that covered. I have a question, Doc!"

"Yes? Can I bring her home and have a doctor here on call for her?"

"Well yes, if you can afford to have one and supply her with meds, IV, and any other necessities that she may need, you can."

"Okay! Do you have a referral slip of certified doctors?"

"Well yes, Jayson, I will have that ready when you come by."

"Well, I will be there in about an hour." Jayson made a couple of calls to some friends he had and let them know that he was looking for two female nurses to come to his home to help out with Sheryl. Jayson knew that it would be too much for the nanny to take care of Montero and Sheryl at the same time; he wanted the nanny's attention strictly on Montero.

Jayson said to himself. *It would be better for all of us if we could have Sheryl home, then Montero can spend more time with his mom, and she will be home when he wakes up.* Everything was working out just fine for Jayson. It's not like he couldn't afford to pay for what Sheryl needed to get better. Jayson missed Sheryl very much. He continued to talk to her as if she could hear him. You never know, maybe she could, we don't know it. But it's now getting stressful; Sheryl had been in a coma for almost a month.

Sixth-Month Celebration

Montero was turning six months in just one more week. Jayson considered Montero his son, and no one could tell him differently. He's planning a sixth-month party for Montero. He got a few people to help him. Jayson didn't know much about a kids' party, but he would make sure that it's something that Montero would never forget. Montero started to crawl all over the place; everything that he did, Jayson made sure that he recorded it so Sheryl wouldn't miss a thing.

One of the nurses that Jayson hired wasn't doing a good job with Sheryl, and she was constantly in Jayson's face. Jayson sat her down one day to talk to her about the services she was giving and that he was not satisfied. He also let her know that he realized the flirting she was doing toward him and that he wasn't interested. He also let her know that if she's there for him, she needed to go, she was no longer needed. Jayson told her that all the focus in the house was needed to be on Sheryl.

The nurse's name was Angie. When Jayson told Angie that at all of the focus was on Sheryl, she immediately got up and stood in front of Jayson and said, "Don't you think you need some attention too? I mean you've been taking care of her for months now. Who's taking care of you?"

Jayson got up from the table and told Angie to pack her things and leave his home. She pleaded with him that she was only trying to help him. He responded to her and told her that he didn't need her help and there was only one woman for him.

He walked away from Angie and went upstairs where Sheryl was. He gave Sheryl a kiss on her cheek and told her that he would be back shortly, that he had to go find another helper for her. Jayson walked downstairs to see Angie was still sitting there. Jayson called security to make sure that Angie was off the premises before he left; he let the guard know that she was not wanted back on the property. Jayson found an older person that he thought would be better to help him with Sheryl and the party for his future son.

He also needed to find a suitable child care provider. His former sitter no longer wanted to keep Montero after hearing what Roger had done to Sheryl. She feared what could happen to her. Jayson didn't have a problem with it, and he understood where she was coming from. Everything seemed to go wrong, but Jayson never gave up. He did everything that he had to do for Sheryl; he really wanted her to get better.

Looking for Help

A good help is hard to find. Jayson decided to put an ad in the paper for a responsible person to sit with Montero for only three hours a day, four days a week. To Jayson, it seemed like everyone that answered his ad was only after him and had no concern for what he really wanted. His mother told him to release his ad from the papers; she would take full responsibility for Sheryl until she was 100 percent better. Jayson agreed. Jayson's mother didn't move in with them. She just made it her business to be there. If Jayson did decide to hire someone other than his mother, she would be there to make sure everything was in order. It took Jayson a few days to find a suitable sitter for Montero while he's at work. He found an older woman named Christine. She's well known for her experience in palliative care, who was the best person for Sheryl at this point. Jayson's mom took the job of taking care of Montero while Christine would take care of Sheryl, being that she had the experience. Jayson was comfortable with Christine and didn't have any problems with her. Everything seemed to be working out just fine.

CHAPTER 18

Sheryl Moves

A couple of weeks had passed it's now time for Montero's party in two more days. Sheryl moved only one of her fingers and twitched her eyes, but no one noticed because it always happened briefly. It's been six months, and two weeks since Sheryl was in a coma. What a faithful and caring man Jayson really was. He believed in his heart that Sheryl was his soul mate, and the way he treated Sheryl, you would believe that they were more than friends. It's Saturday, time to have Montero's birthday party. Jayson didn't invite that much kids over to the house for the party.

Twenty-five kids and twelve adults! He wanted to keep it to a minimum. He didn't want much people plundering on the property or making excessive amount of noise, so he kept it at a small and sensible. It's now time for the party in seven hours; Jayson was getting everything ready for Montero. The party had now been going on about an hour now. Jayson recorded everything that Montero did so Sheryl won't miss any part of his childhood. It's now four o'clock in the afternoon; everyone was eating out on the patio.

Getting Up

Sheryl was upstairs sitting on the edge of the bed. She's very weak at this point. She stood up and, with not much strength, made it into the hall, holding on to the railing of the stairs. Sheryl took one step at a time. She's walking slowly with only five more steps to go. Sheryl saw small children running around in the yard playing. She made it to the patio door; she scared the housekeeper by walking up behind her. The housekeeper yelled, "Ayah!" Everyone looked back to see what had happened. No one saw Sheryl yet, she was coming out of the house, and she got weak and couldn't make another step. The housekeeper yelled for Jayson; he immediately ran toward her and asked her what's wrong. The housekeeper moved to the side, and Sheryl was standing in the doorway. Jayson didn't waste any time. He ran to Sheryl, hugging her, but he felt when her knees buckled. "You're weak. I need to take you back upstairs."

"No," said Sheryl, "what's going on out here?"

"Well, its Montero's birthday today, and we're celebrating it for him. Don't worry, you didn't miss a thing. I have recorded everything you should see." Sheryl struggled. "That's it," said Jayson. "You're going back to bed; you're not strong enough to be out of bed." Sheryl didn't want to go back upstairs to get in bed. Jayson picked her up and took her upstairs to her room. He put Sheryl back into bed. Jayson immediately called the doctor to let him know what was going on. The doctor came over to check Sheryl's vital signs and blood pressure. He let Jayson know that Sheryl would have to come down to the office to get a CT scan the next day to see what they could do about the blood clot she had in her occipital area. While the doctor was still talking to Jayson, Sheryl slipped back into coma. Jayson grabbed her hands; he started shaking her calling out, "Sheryl, Sheryl, please, baby." He then started to pray, "Lord, please help her. We need her here." Sheryl moved only one finger; they knew it wouldn't be long before she woke up.

Jayson stayed with Sheryl more than he stayed at the office or home. He didn't want to leave Sheryl side. The doctor let Jayson know that the blood clot would have to come out in order for her not to go into another coma; he said that the clot was putting pressure on her brain.

Jayson was barely eating, worrying himself sickly about Sheryl, thinking what he could really do to help her.

By Your Side

Jayson won't leave her side again no matter what he had to do. He went downstairs to get Montero; he moved the playpen in Sheryl's room. He would sleep with Sheryl in her bed, hugging her every night and making sure that she stayed comfortable.

Jayson cared for Sheryl very much. She meant the world to him, and protecting her was his first priority.

Awoke

It was the third day after she slipped back into a light coma. Jayson would put his leg underneath Sheryl's legs while sleeping. He felt movements but didn't get excited because he knew that it could be just a muscle reaction. The lights were off, and it's two o'clock in the morning. He continued to feel movement. He finally took a chance and called out, "Sheryl, are you awake?"

"Yes, and what are you doing in my bed?"

"I wanted to be here when you woke up."

"Why?"

"It'll be all right. Here, lie down for now."

"No!" said Sheryl. "I am hungry I can eat a whole chicken."

"Okay then," said Jayson. Jayson called down to the cook and told Mildred, that's her name, to fix Sheryl something to eat.

Mildred said, "Are you serious, and is she up?"

Jayson answered with the sound of happiness in his voice, "Yes, she's awake."

Mildred immediately ran up to see for herself. "Oh! Sheryl, we have missed you so much. How are you feeling?"

"I feel great, I feel like I was working for sixteen hours, but other than that, I'm good. Where's my food?"

"Give me just a few minutes, and I will have you something right up." Mildred went downstairs. She picked up the phone and called Trisha, Jayson's mom, and told her what's going on. She came from the guesthouse; somewhere she loved to stay in from time to time. She didn't awake Montero. Mildred met her at the door.

"Come on in. Jayson's up there with her, talking to her. He won't leave the room!" Trisha walked upstairs, knocked on the door, and called out to Jayson and Sheryl.

"Come in, Momma," said Sheryl.

"How are you feeling?" asked Trisha.

"I'm feeling okay. My stomach feels kind of empty like I haven't eaten anything."

"No! You haven't," said Trisha.

Jayson told his mom to go down to help Mildred before she would blurt out what really happened to Sheryl. Jayson didn't want Sheryl to worry about that right now. He just wanted her to have a good morning on a positive note. It wasn't long before Sheryl needed to get up to use the bathroom. But Jayson couldn't allow her to do that until the nurse got there the next day because of the urine sac she had to tote on her side. She felt it as she tried to get out of the bed. She patted herself on the side where she felt the lump. "What is this?"

"Sheryl, please don't be alarmed."

"What is this?" she asked again. Jayson told her that she had been sick.

"Sick of what?" Sheryl asked again. "Jayson, what is this?" Sheryl immediately streamed downstairs for Jayson's mom. "What happened to me?" She was frantically yelling. "Why do I have this thing on me? What happened?"

Trisha looked at Jayson. "Did you tell her?"

Jayson shook his head no. "I didn't."

"Tell me what? What is going on? What happened? Why is this thing on me?"

CHAPTER 19

The Explanation

Trisha said, "Baby, something happened to you a few months ago."

"Wait," said Sheryl. "What do you mean a few months ago? What happened yesterday or last week for that matter. What do you mean a few months ago?" Sheryl tried to get up quickly but slouched slightly on the bed. "Whoa! Why do I feel weak? What kind of sickness did I have?"

Jayson was always the person who liked to keep conflict down? He didn't want to tell Sheryl right now, but if he didn't tell her, she probably won't trust him and leave. So he told her to eat her dinner and that he will tell her everything she needed to know. Sheryl agreed because she was so ready to eat something.

Jayson sat in the chair and watched Sheryl as she was eating her dinner. Sheryl saw the hurt in Jayson's eyes. She asked Jayson, "What is really bothering you?"

"I love you," Jayson said to Sheryl.

"You what?" answered Sheryl. "Are you sick too?"

Jayson replied, "Yes, I am."

Sheryl asked Jayson, "Why are you sick?"

Jayson responded, "I'm sick of not being there for you, I'm sick of you hurting, and I'm sick because I didn't protect you the day you got hurt. Sheryl, I care for you too much not to let you know what happened to you."

Sheryl dropped her plate. "What happened to me, Jayson?"

Jayson started to cry. He got up and went to Sheryl and gave her a hug and reassured her that he would be there by her side from now on no matter what. He promised that he would take care of everything. Sheryl got real worried; she thought that she was dying. So Sheryl asked, "Well, am I dying or something?"

"No baby You're not dying? It's just the beginning of a new life for you, I promise." Jayson stood in front of Sheryl and asked her, "Do you trust me?"

"Yes," Sheryl answered.

"No, I really need to know if you really trust me with your life."

"Yes, I honestly do. I trust you enough to be around my baby."

"Your baby," Jayson replied.

"Yes, my baby."

"Well, Sheryl!"

Sheryl had gotten frantic. "What happened to Montero?"

"Calm down, Sheryl, nothing happened to him! He's just not a baby anymore."

"What do you mean, Jayson, he's only two and a half months." Tears just fell out of Jayson's eyes.

"No, Sheryl, that's not true. Montero is now turning six months old."

"What in the hell are you talking about? I had him, and you're trying to tell me his age. Where's my son?" Sheryl tried to walk, but she's too weak.

"He's asleep, Sheryl."

"Please I want to see my son."

"You just said you trust me, and I promised you that I will tell you everything. Do you trust me?"

"Yes, but."

"No but! Sit down and let me talk to you. Sheryl sat down with a sad look on her face, just waiting to hear what Jayson had to tell her. Jayson grabbed both of Sheryl's hands, and he told her how he felt about her. He told her that he's going to take care of her and Montero. Jayson continued to tell her that she had missed out on the physical things in Montero's life, but he had pictures and video, so she could see what she hadn't seen. "Something bad happened to you some months back, and it's not good. Sheryl, you've been attacked and badly beaten."

"What?"

"Please, Sheryl, you promise that you would stay calm. We are here for you, and I don't know how many times I have to tell you that I will take care of you and Montero."

"Please, Jayson, tell me who attacked me."

"Sheryl, it's not a stranger."

"Who did this?"

"It was Roger."

"Roger, Roger. What are you talking about, is he here?"

"Yes, Sheryl, but he's not in jail right now."

"How could he do this to me? How did he know where I was, we are in danger. Did he hurt my son?"

"No, sweetheart, he was with the sitter." Jayson hugged Sheryl; he didn't want to let her go because he knew the next thing Sheryl would do was go to the mirror. Jayson was not ready for that.

To See My Face

Sheryl pulled away from Jayson. She paced really slowly to the bathroom. Jayson tried to stop her from going into the bathroom, but he didn't want to force her not to look. Jayson pleaded with her to wait a few weeks for her face to heal, but Sheryl would not listen, she really wanted to see what the big argument was about. She looked in the mirror, and she screamed as if someone had pierced her in her side. She fell to the floor crying, "What had he done to me?"

Montero came in the room, calling, "Daddy, Daddy." Sheryl quickly shut the bathroom door.

"Please, I can't let my son see me like this. Take him out of here, Jayson." Sheryl was crying, "I can't let my son see me like this." Jayson told the nanny to take Montero with her, and she did. Jayson stayed in Sheryl's room for hours talking to her, telling her that he's very sorry for not being there.

Sheryl said, "It's not your fault. I blame you for nothing, you have done a lot, more than I can ever imagine." Jayson told Sheryl that he needed to call the doctor so he could get her to the hospital as soon as possible and that they could give her a CT scan of her brain to see what they needed to do. Sheryl agreed.

They went to the hospital the next morning, and Jayson didn't move an inch. He wanted to be there to hear everything that the doctor had to say. The doctors came in Sheryl's room to give her the results of her CT scan. When they came in, they didn't look excited at all. Jayson grabbed Sheryl's hands. "Think positive, baby. Don't worry; it's going to be all right."

"Well, Ms. Sheryl, we don't see a reason to keep you. We don't know what happened to the clot, but it's gone. Your vitals are fine. The only thing we would like to know is when you want us to set your appointment for your surgery for your face."

"My face?" said Sheryl.

"Yes, we want to make the correction so you can have a normal life. It's not that serious and you won't have to stay in the hospital overnight."

"That's great," said Sheryl.

"Let's set it for next week, Wednesday."

"That'll be great," Sheryl said. It's hard for Sheryl not seeing her son or holding him. She had to do things with Montero when he's asleep. She didn't want him to see her face the way it is, badly scared. Sheryl cried a lot in her sleep. She grasped Jayson real tight and told him to hold her and not let her go. Jayson held her hands as they walked out of the hospital. He opened the car door for Sheryl; she got in and they proceeded to the house. Sheryl went upstairs in Montero's room. She kissed him while he was sleeping. Jayson called her out of the room and told her that she needed to be with him when he's up. He's still young and he wouldn't really pay attention to the scar on her face.

Chapter 20

The Scars

Sheryl tried to play with Montero while he's awake a couple of times, but it really hurt her when Montero pinched at her scars. She didn't want to experience that again. Sheryl let Jayson know that he was a perfect stranger in her life and that she really appreciated him so much. Jayson told Sheryl that they needed to talk about her safety because they hadn't found Roger yet. He's out there somewhere. "It doesn't really matter," Sheryl said. "He won't be charged with anything major. He has friends in high places, and he probably won't serve any time."

"Sheryl, that's attempted murder."

"That doesn't matter, Jayson. He will get off, and I promise you, I'm not safe no matter what I do. Roger will find me, and next time, he may kill me. Do you understand what I'm saying?"

"Let's not talk about that right now," replied Jayson. "Let's just focus on you getting better, and then we will decide where we will go."

"No!" said Sheryl. "You will not leave your home for me."

"I'll do whatever it takes to make you happy, that's all that matters to me right now. What about your mother and your family?"

"Sheryl, listen, sweetheart, they have their own lives, I'm just starting mine. I have someone that I care for deeply, and I finally have a son."

"Jayson, I won't let you take on the responsibility of taking care of me and my son."

"Sheryl, it's not by coincidence that you and I met on the beach. I believe things happen for a reason. Just out of the blue, you chose Jamaica to rest or to have a peace of mind and for your vacation, think about it. We are destined to be together, don't you think? Where I'm from, we believe in family. We believe in taking care of our madam, and you belong here with me."

"Jayson, I'm not ready for another relationship. I just met you just a few months ago, and I'm very comfortable with you, but remember, I was also comfortable with a man I've been with for fifteen years, and look what happen to me. I trust no one anymore," Sheryl said, crying. "I am sorry, but look at me, my face is damaged. Who would have thought that this would happen to me? I'm not pretty anymore."

"Stop it," said Jayson. "Enough of the negativity you got going on. Look at me, Sheryl. There's more to you than outer beauty. You are beautiful regardless what your face looks like. We know what happened. Your heart is beautiful, and that's all I want. Your heart! Your face will heal to where it once was, I promise you that. I stress over and over again how I feel about you and Montero. I stress how much I want to be with you and that I will protect you both. You said that you trust and believe in me. But all I'm seeing and feeling is doubt. Why? Sheryl, the worst is over. You can't let Roger take control of your life, our life, our life together."

Trusting

"Trust me and give me a chance to show you how much I do love you and Montero. You know what, let's end this conversation. I want you to lie down and breathe easy. I want you to get some rest right now. I have to check on Montero. Come on, I'll help you upstairs. Come on, Sheryl, I don't like arguing at all. Let me get you an extra pillow."

"Okay," said Sheryl. Sheryl went into her room and lay down.

The kiss

Jayson came in and gave her the extra pillows. He kissed Sheryl on her cheek. Sheryl looked up and told Jayson, "I know exactly what that means."

"What are you talking about?" asked Jayson. Sheryl answered Jayson and said,

"When a man kisses a woman on the cheek, it means you love and care for her. Is that true?"

"Well yes, madam! How did you know about that?"

"I studied this country because, remember, this is where I wanted to come for my second honeymoon. I also know that if you kiss a lady on the lips and her forehead in the same kiss, you truly love her and want to marry her."

"That's great," said Jayson. "Now get some rest. I'll be back shortly." Jayson went out to find that perfect ring for his future wife. He didn't want to wait any longer. He wanted to marry Sheryl, and nothing else mattered.

CHAPTER 21

Surgery Prep

It's time for Sheryl to go to her first visit for her surgery. Jayson took Montero to the sitter down the street. His mom had an appointment, and she couldn't keep him today. It took the doctors about five hours just to prep Sheryl. With the change of plans, she had to stay in the hospital, and they could start her surgery at five o'clock in the morning. Jayson stayed by Sheryl's side no matter what; he was constantly calling the sitter. He felt better when his mom said that she would pick Montero up from the sitter and take him home. It's now three o'clock in the afternoon, and Sheryl was now asleep. Jayson wanted to go home to see about his son; he missed him and hadn't seen him in ten hours. Jayson went to pick up Montero from out of the playpen. He took him upstairs to bathe him, made sure that he ate, and played with him for a while, and wanted to tuck him in before he went to see Sheryl at the hospital. It's now one hour before Montero was put down for a nap. Jayson decided to get on the floor with Montero to play with him. With Jayson lying on his back and Montero in the air as the airplane, he was laughing and playing, just having fun with his dad.

The Police Officer

While playing on the floor for the last twenty minutes, Jayson then heard very clearly music to his ear for the first time. He's swinging Montero over his head, and the words that came out of Montero's mouth were, "Daddy, look!" Jayson was astounded.

He asked, "What did you say?" Montero laughed. A tear fell from Jayson's eyes. Montero touched his face and said, "Dada, look," and he pointed toward the door. Jayson immediately looked up and saw two police officers standing at his door. He jumped up and put Montero in the playpen. He walked toward the door and slid the door open and asked the officers. "May I help you?"

"Jayson Colbert."

"Yes!" answered Jayson!

"We need you down to the hospital right away."

"Why?" Jayson asked. "Is everything all right? What's going on?"

"Well, Roger was caught trying to take Sheryl from the hospital."

"What? Where is Sheryl?"

"She's fine, Mr. Colbert. We just need to get there right away."

"Well, my son is with me, I just picked him up from the sitter's and I have to take him with me."

"That will be fine," responded the officers. "I will bring in a female officer to watch him."

"That won't be necessary," stated Jayson. "I'm taking my son with me." The officer waited while Jayson strapped his son in the seat of the car. Jayson was not fully dressed, but he didn't care at this point. There was only one important thing that was on Jayson mind, and that was Sheryl. He just wanted to get to the hospital to see Sheryl. They made it to the hospital, and Jayson strapped Montero in front of him, going up in the elevator. He waited for the door to open. Doors opening, he ran quickly down the hall to Sheryl's room. "Baby, are you all right?" Sheryl was sitting; there with a smile on her face. When Jayson walked in, he expected Sheryl to be in a terrible state of fear. But that's not what Jayson saw when he walked in. He immediately asked the policeman what kind of joke they were playing.

Officer Taylor said, "This is not a joke or a game, we don't know why Sheryl is smiling with happiness. We will stand outside. If you need us, we're here." The officers walked out of Sheryl's room. Jayson turned to Sheryl and asked her, "What's going on because the cops came to the house all frantic about Roger."

"Yes," said Sheryl, "which is true."

"Well, why are you smiling about that?" Sheryl looked up at Jayson and said, "I'm glad Roger came to my room."

"What are you talking about?" asked Jayson.

"Just hear me out, Jayson."

Feelings

She began to talk to Jayson and told him what she saw outside of her window and how she really felt.

Sheryl had great feelings for Jayson. But she was scared to show that love and affection. Sheryl told Jayson when he left earlier; she turned over, looking out of the widow. She saw a white dove sitting on the first limb in the tree just above the window. She said a short prayer and asked God, "What does this mean? Are you really trying to tell me something? What is really going on?" She told Jayson that she felt at ease when the dove flew away. She fell asleep and was resting very well for the first time really since she's been there. Without any dreams or bad thoughts! "I thought that I wasn't ready for a relationship, but truly I am! I'm ready to live and to be loved. I'm ready to be happy. I just need to work on some things right now. So I want to take it slow, and I'm not making any promises or commitment. Let's just say that we are going on a few dates."

"Sounds good to me," stated Jayson. Jayson knew that it's only a matter of time when Sheryl would come around for something more serious than dating. He knew that. Jayson didn't want to spoil a great day, but he had to tell Sheryl what he was about to do.

Court Day

"Roger had his court hearing today. And I'm going to see what the outcome of it will be."

"Are you sure?" Sheryl asked Jayson.

"Yes, I'm sure, I won't be long. I'll be back as soon as possible." Jayson made his way to the courthouse, hoping to bring Sheryl some good news back.

The Hearing

Just as Sheryl said, Roger didn't get much time at all. Three months and probation! That's nothing. *I don't know how to tell Sheryl this.* No need for him to tell Sheryl that. Sheryl already knew. She looked at the news, and there was Roger with that funny smirk on his face as if he knew something they didn't. Jayson worried how Sheryl would react when he told her about the verdict. Jayson walked in the room to let Sheryl know what happened in court. Sheryl said to Jayson, "Don't even worry about it."

Jayson looked at Sheryl with amazement because he didn't know what to think and why Sheryl said that. But she immediately told Jayson, "I know what the verdict is." Jayson then started apologizing.

"What are you apologizing for?" asked Sheryl. "I'm not going to let Roger run my life of me fearing him. I'm going to live and take care of my son. I will no longer hide or run from anybody anymore." Jayson couldn't believe it, but he loved it. Sheryl was really stepping out of her shell.

It's now time for Sheryl to rest a little, to get prepared for her first surgery in the morning. Jayson, no matter what, didn't want anyone in Sheryl's room without his permission; there were still two guards at her door. The time had come for Sheryl to have her surgery. And now in the recovery room waiting for her to rise was no other than Jayson. It wasn't twenty minutes then Sheryl woke up and couldn't smile much because of the mask on her face. But Jayson knew she would if she could. Jayson held Montero over Sheryl so he could give her a kiss on the cheek. Montero kissed his mom on both sides of her cheeks. Sheryl fought for that smile and slowly said to Jayson, "I see he's learning quickly." Sheryl was able to return home after three days of rest and evaluation.

CHAPTER 22

Going Home

Jayson was taking care of Sheryl like no other. He's constantly there for her. He tucked Sheryl in as the housekeeper prepared a light diet for Sheryl. "I'll be right back; I'm going downstairs to check on your meal." Before Jayson left the room, he bent down and kissed Sheryl on both sides of her cheeks, her forehead, and her nose. Jayson slowly walked away.

Sheryl asked, "What does that mean?"

He looked back at Sheryl, began to walk up to the bedside, and kissed her directly on the lips, holding that kiss for a few seconds, and whispered to her. "You will find out soon enough." Sheryl saw Jayson's mother heading to Montero's room and said, "Mum, what does it mean when a man kiss you on both side of your cheek, your forehead, then your nose, walk away, comes back, and kiss you on the lips with great pressure?"

With tears falling from Jayson's mother's eyes, finally she said, "Finally."

"What?" asked Sheryl?

"That's not my place to tell you, that's his place, dear."

"Oh! Please tell me. I won't tell him that you have told me."

"No," responded Jayson's mother. "I will do no such thing. That is dishonesty, and we don't allow dishonesty in this family. You have to wait your turn." She patted Sheryl on her back and said. "Your time's soon to come, just be patient." Sheryl continued to bust her brains trying to figure out what it means.

But she could not get the answer to her question, and no one would give any information. Wouldn't she like to know the secret? If she really paid any attention to Jayson, she could really figure out what was really going on. Sheryl gave up and decided to wait on Jayson to let her in on what's been really going on with all these secret codes.

Going out

A few weeks had passed and Jayson was tired of Sheryl home not doing anything. So he wanted to take her out to get her some fresh air. Jayson went upstairs to ask Sheryl if she wanted to go out for a little bit, just to get out of the house. "I guess it would be okay, that'll be fine," said Sheryl.

"We'll be leaving at seven thirty sharp."

"Okay, that's fine," replied Sheryl. Little did Sheryl know when Jayson left her earlier, he went to reserve a table at the best restaurant and gave a two-carat diamond ring to the waiter to slip in her glass of wine with four dozen roses for the night. Sheryl was getting ready for her special night out for the first time in months. Jayson sent a limo for Sheryl about 6:45 p.m., which was unexpected. Sheryl looked with amazement. "Wow!" She proceeded to get into the car, not knowing where she's going. But the driver Dan knew where Jayson wanted her to go.

They were now driving for about ten minutes. Sheryl looked around. "It's beautiful out here." All Sheryl saw was a bunch of lights, flowers, and palm trees. "Where are we going, sir?"

Dan responded, "We're almost there!" and pulled up to the doorway of a three-storey building. Couples on each side dropped shiny things like gold petals on the ground in front of her. She stood there with amazement, looking around for Jayson. Sheryl didn't see him; she continued to walk up the stairs. Three ladies were dropping rose petals. "Now," said Sheryl, "this is just a bit much."

"Not for you, madam." Sheryl looked up into Jayson's eyes. "You're here!"

"Yes," said Jayson, "waiting for you. Come let's enter for dinner." Sheryl and Jayson proceeded to walk to their table.

"My god," said Sheryl. "This is beautiful. Why did you do all of this?"

"Well," responded Jayson, "This is a special day in my life, and I want to share it with you."

"Did you get a promotion or something?" asked Sheryl.

"No. Its way better than that," Jayson responded. Sheryl wanted to ask another question, but the waiter walked up, waiting to take their order. Jayson placed their orders. Jayson excused himself from the dinner table. "I have to go to the men's room." He went into the kitchen to make sure everything was in order. Jayson's family was at the back with the cooks in the waiting area. Jayson planned for his family to come out when Sheryl drank her wine and spotted the ring. Jayson proceeded back to the table. "Are you okay?" he asked Sheryl.

"Yes, I'm great," Sheryl responded. The waiter with their food and drinks.

An orchestra came around the table and played a soft melody for Sheryl. Sheryl started to tear up. "How sweet, I've never felt so special in my life. This is beautiful, I feel like a Nubian queen," said Sheryl.

"That's what you are to me," responded Jayson. "This is just the beginning."

"What do you mean?" asked Sheryl.

"Let's just enjoy our dinner, and let nature take its course." Sheryl smiled. Jayson led the prayer, and they began to eat.

"Uhm," said Sheryl, "what did you order? This is great." Jayson gave her the name of the meat she was eating in his terms. It sounded exquisite; she said it's good. Jayson asked her if she knew what that means.

"What is it?" asked Sheryl.

"It's curry goat with potatoes, mushrooms, and onions."

Sheryl looked at Jayson. "What? Are you serious?"

"Yes!" She continued to eat her dinner. She took a sip of her wine, gazing her eyes into Jayson's.

CHAPTER 23

Let's Dance

He asked Sheryl to dance. Sheryl said in a soft voice, "I wish I could remember how to." She stood closely in front of Jayson. She stepped on his feet, and she quickly got discouraged and began to walk away. He grabbed Sheryl from behind, putting both hands around her waist, turning her around quickly. Jayson said in a sensual voice, "I'll take it from here." Jayson slowly took Sheryl's hands and placed it around his neck, slowly caressing her body. She loved that feeling of security. But she got a little afraid of making a mistake. The song was slowly going off as Jayson danced Sheryl back to her seat.

"Thank you," said Sheryl.

"I'm having a great time here!" said Jayson. "Let's have a little more wine."

"Okay!" responded Sheryl. Jayson poured very little in the glass so Sheryl could see the ring. He told Sheryl they would toast to positive things in life.

She smiled and said to Jayson, "I'm praying for that."

They toast, and Sheryl took a sip of her wine, seeing this bright shine at the bottom. "Jayson, something's in my wine." Right then, Jayson's family came out. Sheryl said, "What are you doing here?"

"We're just having dinner here, can we join you?"

"Sure," said Sheryl. Jayson called the waiter to remove Sheryl's glass from the table. The waiter returned with the ring cleaned up in a white satin handkerchief and handed it to Jayson along with the microphone.

Jayson stood up. "Sheryl, you are everything I have dreamed of, you have a son that I adore. I've always wanted a son, and I love him to death. I've never been married or in a serious relationship. I know you care for me, and I for you, there's something I want to ask you."

Sheryl stopped Jayson. "Not in front everyone."

"Yes! I'm not ashamed, and I have nothing to hide." Jayson proceeded to ask her how she really felt for him. Sheryl looked at Jayson with a glossy look in her eyes.

"I, uhm, uhm! I fear a lot of things, but I don't want to be careful with the person I'm with or be afraid to talk to him. I'm tired of fighting myself not to love you. I'm in it so deep for you, but afraid to open that door. You are a wonderful man, you make a great dad. I just don't want to make you suffer for what I'm feeling inside at times."

Jayson said, "Stop, Sheryl," holding her hands with nervousness. "Sheryl, how do you feel about me?"

Sheryl held her head down and looked back up at Jayson. "I love you like no other. Even throughout the years when I thought I knew love and had real love, I really didn't. What I'm feeling now is totally different. I love you very much!"

"Okay," said Jayson. "If you strongly feel that way, Sheryl, and you have no doubt in your mind that we can make this work between us, will you marry me?" Sheryl bust out with tears, asking Jayson if he was sure he wanted a ready-made family. "I have a lot of things, I need to—"

Before Sheryl could finish her sentence, Jayson placed two of his fingers across Sheryl's lips and said, "I know you and your son, I love you both."

Will You Marry Me?

"I want to marry you, will you be my wife?"

"Yes! Yes, Jayson," Sheryl cried for the rest of the night. An hour had passed but she was still crying. She held her head down. Jayson lifted her head up, got on his knees, and told her what she really meant to him.

The Urge

Even though Jayson's a virgin, he had the urge also. But he only wanted his wife to have him. No matter what! Jayson never gave in. He not only respected himself, but he also respected Sheryl and her body. It seemed like two months was a long time before Sheryl and Jayson shared their vows. The closer it gets, the more Sheryl feared the word *marriage*, even though Sheryl hadn't heard from Roger. She still didn't let her guard down.

Roger heard about the wedding through the newspaper. He wanted to stop the wedding but didn't know how. Jayson didn't want to cause any worry to Sheryl, so he kept everything quiet until after the wedding. Jayson wanted their lives to be based on happiness, but he knew that he couldn't keep something like that from Sheryl. Sheryl often thought about Jayson never been married or in a serious relationship. She didn't want him to experience something she's going through or have him dealing with Roger's drama. That's the biggest thing Sheryl was worried about.

Things didn't get any better. When Sheryl checked the mail, there was a letter from Roger telling her he wanted his son or she would be sorry. She immediately took the letter to Jayson's at his office. "What's wrong, Sheryl?"

"He knows."

"He who?" asked Jayson. She handed Jayson the letter from Roger.

"Oh! Sheryl, please don't let this worry you, he can't come here. He's posted all over."

"I just don't want any trouble," said Sheryl. "He can't come, but he can send someone to take my son."

"True enough," said Jayson. "We'll go to the police station, show them this letter, and they would have more security here. When we get married, where you want to go on our honeymoon? We can move there."

"No! I feel safer with you and your family."

"Okay then, we will stay here and be a family. Don't fear, my queen, I give my word to my father and you that no one would hurt you ever again. Now let's go handle this. I promise you, you are safe."

Sheryl looked up at Jayson and said, "I believe every word you say to me. I've never felt so much security. I just don't want my troubles to follow me here to destroy your life."

Jayson assured Sheryl that everything would be fine, and she kissed him and let him know that she would go home to start dinner for the two of them. Jayson kissed Sheryl and told her to have a great day.

Sheryl proceeded to her car and went home. She waited for Jayson to come from work. Jayson came in an hour early. "Wow, you home early."

"Yes," said Jayson. "We only have a couple of weeks left before we are married, and I needed to get some things together."

"Oh, okay," said Sheryl. "We have rehearsal tomorrow at seven. So you think you will get off early enough for us to make it?"

"Baby, I won't be going into work for the rest of the week for that matter, not until after our honeymoon."

"That's great," said Sheryl.

"We can spend the next two days together."

"I would love that greatly," said Sheryl. They continued out the day talking and laughing, telling bad jokes and playing practical jokes on each other.

The day had passed they were now coming back from their rehearsal dinner smiling and happy as ever.

A few weeks had gone by. "Well, Sheryl, it's less than twenty-four hours, and you will be my wife."

"Oh yes, and the closer it gets to that time, the more I'm feeling a little shaky and scared."

"Don't be," said Jayson. "I'm much afraid as you are, but we are here together for each other. We will both do well. Are you afraid to say your own vows?"

"Well, I thought we were going to repeat what the pastor say," answered Sheryl.

"That's too traditional. I believe we need to say what's in our heart. What I feel for you, Sheryl, is more than repeating the words of a traditional saying."

"Well okay," said Sheryl, "I can do it because what I feel is so much more than what I hear them say anyway." They both had a little fear, not of each other, but the feeling of finally finding that love they both were waiting for.

It's now seven thirty, and Jayson's friends came over to take him out. Jayson knew that they wanted to take him to a bachelor party, and he knew that there would be strippers. Jayson told his friends that he wasn't interested in doing anything like that, and the only body he wanted to see was Sheryl's tomorrow night.

They didn't like it, but they respected his wishes. So they proceeded on to their night of fun, without girls.

CHAPTER 24

The Wedding Day

It's time for the wedding day, and everyone's getting ready. Sheryl was still sleeping in her bed with only four hours before the wedding. Jayson's mother walked in and asked Sheryl why she was still in bed. Sheryl was shaking with nervousness, crying and telling her that she was scared to go out there and that she didn't know what to do. She reminded Sheryl that this was the best time of her life and Jayson really loved her. It made Sheryl feel a lot better when she said that Sheryl was her daughter, and she's honored to be her mother-in-law. Sheryl gave her a big hug and told her thank-you. She then got up and pulled herself together and got ready for her wedding. Sheryl didn't have any friends and didn't know anyone, so she used her nanny, the housekeeper, Senate, and a couple of the housekeepers to be the bridesmaids. She had Jayson's mother to be her maid of honor. Jayson hadn't seen or talked to Sheryl since eight o'clock the night before. He's now ready to be with her. It's been a long time for the both of them sexually. Jayson haven't had sex at all in his lifetime.

Sheryl had been living with Jayson for almost two years and not having any sexual encounter of her own since she had left Roger. You must really know how they feel. Everyone was waiting in the church. Jayson and his groomsmen arrived, getting in place. It's now Sheryl's turn to come down the aisle! Here came the maid of honor (Jayson's mother), flower girls, and the ring bearer. The wedding theme was played for Sheryl to make her entrance. No Sheryl. Sheryl was at the door fretting for Jayson. His mother came out of the church to talk to Sheryl. She was crying, telling her that there were a lot of people in there and that she's afraid. "I'm with you, and Jayson is waiting for you, so please come." Sheryl was crying and shaking horrifically. Jayson's mom comforted her by telling her, "These people don't know you. Do you know how much women I had to run away from my son? You are the first woman that I loved in my son's life. Come on, Sheryl; just keep your eyes on Jayson, no one else. Come on, you can do this."

Sheryl finally made her way to the altar where Jayson was. She turned to him. He unveiled her and grabbed her hand, squeezing it softly, giving her a wink. They proceeded into the ceremony. They shared their vows as they said they would. During Jayson's vows, Sheryl didn't expect Jayson to cry but he did. That hit a soft spot in Sheryl. She kissed Jayson on the lips and said its okay; they were now pronounced husband and wife. They were having the time of their lives at the wedding reception. Jayson danced with Sheryl two songs straight. They both were ready to leave to start their honeymoon. Jayson told his mom that they would be leaving in the next twenty minutes.

The Honeymoon

They spent time with Montero before they left, thanking everyone for participating in the special occasion of their marriage. They were now on their way to spending the rest of their life together! They had reached their destination and couldn't wait to get in their hotel suite. Jayson, being so romantic, picked Sheryl up and took her across the threshold into the hotel suite. He stood her up in front of the bed and stripped her down while gazing into her eyes. Sheryl looked into Jayson's eyes with sincerity of love that she was feeling, but shaking uncontrollably with nervousness. "It's okay, Sheryl, I'm just as nervous as you are. Let me tell you this, Sheryl, and I have never told you this before, and I'm ashamed of it. But I feel good about it because it's you that I'm sharing my body with."

"What is it?" asked Sheryl.

"I'm a virgin."

"No way," said Sheryl, "but you are thirty-eight years old."

"Yes! I am. I wanted to wait for my wife, only to give myself to her, and now it's you and I'm yours completely. So there's no need for you to be afraid, I have no experience. Maybe you can teach me something."

Sheryl laughed and felt more comfortable. They went into the shower and bathed each other. As they got out of the shower, they decided not to dry off. Jayson guided Sheryl to the bed, laying her down on the end of the bed. He kissed her softly. She said, "Are you sure you're a virgin? It seems to me that you know exactly what you are doing." Jayson talked to Sheryl with a soft voice, whispering in her ear that he loved her very much. He was now kissing her from head to toes, caressing her thighs as he licked between her legs. She moaned very loudly, squeezing his head and sliding her hand up and down his back. He pushed Sheryl farther up on the bed until she reached the middle. Jayson rolled over, putting Sheryl on top. She stuck her tongue in Jayson's ear, slowly taking her tongue and sliding it down his neck onto his chest then stomach, rolling her tongue around his navel. Jayson was quenching and moaning, telling Sheryl that he loved her and it felt so good what she was doing. He then rolled Sheryl over. She's now under Jayson. He's on top, asking Sheryl if she's comfortable with going further. Sheryl, with a little fear of what Jayson had between his legs, being that she had never seen it; Sheryl stuttered and said just to take it slow.

"I will take my time with you," Jayson said as he spread her legs and pulled himself up to the right position to put his dick inside of her. He placed the head of his dick on the top of Sheryl pussy, and she immediately pushed him off and said, "What the fuck do you have there?"

Jayson replied and said, "I won't hurt you, I promise. I will take my time. If I hurt you, let me know and I will stop." Sheryl slowly lay back down. Jayson kissed her and said, "I will never do anything to hurt you." As he talked to her, he got her mind off what he was about to do. She began to talk to him, and when she uttered the first two words "I love" out of her mouth, he pushed his dick in slightly. She squeezed her thigh close, keeping Jayson from going in any further than he did. It felt so good to him he wanted more, so he massaged Sheryl's thighs to relax her, and she loosened up a little more. He was able to slide another inch inside of her. Sheryl started moaning louder. "Am I hurting you?" asked Jayson.

"Yes, just ease up a little, okay!"

"I will stop."

"No!" said Sheryl. "It feels good, just a lot pain."

Jayson wanted to push even more into Sheryl, but he didn't want to scare her on the first night. It was now forty-five minutes into their lovemaking. Jayson saw that Sheryl was getting tired. He asked her if she wanted to stop and take a break. Sheryl said she didn't need a break. He always tried to make Sheryl feel comfortable in every move that he made with her. He asked Sheryl if she could take just a little more of what he had to offer. Not thinking of how dry she's getting and Jayson being as big as he was, not giving any room inside of Sheryl to stay wet. She said yes, but she didn't realize how much package Jayson actually had left to give.

They both were moaning and having a great time together as she talked to Jayson, telling him how good he felt to her, not thinking at that moment. A feeling came over Jayson with a force, and he pushed a little too much inside this time. Sheryl screamed, "Oh my gosh! That hurts."

Jayson apologized and said, "I didn't mean to, baby, I promise I won't push any more than I already have in." Jayson continued to make love to Sheryl.

Sheryl was screaming and moaning, asking Jayson how it felt. "It's so good. I don't want our night to end." Jayson pulled out, and Sheryl thought that was the end of it. Sheryl sat up on the bed, but Jayson pushed her back down, spreading her legs wide, putting his head between her legs, licking on her clitoris softly. She tried to push herself up toward the top of the bed, but he quickly dragged her down to the bottom of the bed, licking her from the top to the bottom of her pussy. She grabbed for anything she could hold on to.

"Uhm! Jayson, uhm! Please." He messaged her greatly with his tongue, sticking it in and out of her vagina. She's was trying to speak but couldn't. The feelings she's going through would not let her utter a word. "Oh shit, oh shit. I'm about to cum." Sheryl couldn't hold on. Jayson immediately went back up top and place his dick inside of Sheryl. With her being wetter than she was earlier, Jayson thought he could slip another inch into Sheryl. "Oh! My God, Oh! My God!" Between the pressure and her climax, she didn't know what to do with herself. Jayson finally, after three hours, screamed out to Sheryl, "Baby, I'm about to nut."

"Me too, baby." The both of them held each other tight and climaxed together.

"Oh, baby, and uhm! I don't know what to say, I thank God for you. I was waiting all my years for my wife and for the lady of my dreams to only have me." Jayson being a little embarrassed about how he expressed himself to Sheryl, he didn't really care anymore. He just let everything go; anything he was feeling came out.

They both shared tears and really expressed how they felt about what just took place and about each other. Jayson grabbed Sheryl and pulled her close to him as they talked for the next hour. Jayson, not used to having sex, loved that feeling he got and wanted to explore more of it. Sheryl told him maybe later. She told Jayson she felt like she was fighting a bull. Jayson laughed and kissed Sheryl with a passionate kiss before they both went to sleep. They didn't get up until eight o'clock that night.

They took a shower together and decided to go out for dinner. They didn't stay long; they decided to go back to their room to spend more time together. They made a call to check on Montero and Jayson's mom; they spoke briefly to the family. They made the conversation short because it was all about them, and they only had a few days left of their honeymoon. Their lives had just begun.

Thanks for reading,

It's been a great pleasure writing this just for you.

Love is what you make of it. You should only share your body with your husband. You will see the greater part of love and what it really is when you're committed only to one person and you both share the same feelings. Love is not a game but sometimes can take you on a real roller coaster.

Written by Jeanette Shaw

If you have any questions or comments, you can contact Jeanette at Jaysbooksoflife@yahoo.com or 1(843)214-3984.

www.ingramcontent.com/pod-product-compliance
Lightning Source LLC
Chambersburg PA
CBHW030409290526
45785CB00004B/1945